Saturday Special

BETTY BROOKE

ARTHUR JAMES, London

First Edition 1987

© Betty Brooke

All rights reserved by the publisher,

ARTHUR JAMES LIMITED
One Cranbourne Road,
London N10 2BT

British Library Cataloguing in Publication Data
Brooke, Betty
Saturday special
1. Christianity
I. Title
200   BR121.2
ISBN 0-85305-286-7

Cover design and illustrations by
AL THOMAS

Typeset and printed by
The Guernsey Press Co. Ltd., Guernsey, Channel Islands

Dedication

To all my Saturday readers who have a Special place in my
affections.

Acknowledgments

Writing and preaching over many years, notes on sources are not always recorded. Where sources have been traced, they are recorded with appropriate credits. Many references and prayers are simply "Anon". Many more used have been written by the author. If any acknowledgment has not been made and the matter is pointed out, the earliest opportunity possible will be taken to include a proper reference.

The texts are quoted from various translations: AV indicates the use of the *Authorised Version,* NIV the *New International Version* and NEB the *New English Bible.*

Al Thomas who drew the pictures is Studio Manager of the Graphic Design section of the *Jersey Evening Post.* A skilled cartoonist, he has worked closely with the author, providing cartoons for her political column.

Contents

The Moment that matters

"Could you explain what you mean by the sacrament of the present moment?" asked a friend who heard me use the phrase. He wanted an explanation of my personal guide to living which in recent years has become important to me.

Let me explain.

The present moment is the only one about which we can do something *in a positive way*.

At this moment I am writing part of this book. When I stop doing that, I will push back my chair, cover the typewriter and leave my study.

I may not, however, get as far as the door. Who knows what might befall me? I might have a heart attack. A 'phone call may give me good news or bad news. In other words, *I* have little or no control over the *next* moment.

Yesterday is past and gone. The mistakes I have made and the decisions at which I arrived are over and done with, and I can only regret what has happened, or rejoice in it. But *this* moment is the most precious of all. I feel it as I speak to someone, as I listen to someone, as I encounter life's problems. I want to live this moment to the full. It is that feeling which makes it a sacrament.

The person to whom I am speaking is important. The loveliness of the view at which I am looking is all-embracing. Tomorrow it will be different, just as it was different yesterday. I must grasp *this* moment with both hands.

I have given you my personal philosophy. It is what I believe. As I grasp this moment with both hands, I thank God for a sacrament. This is the moment that matters.

Teach us to number our days aright that we may gain a heart of wisdom

Psalm 90, verse 12. (NIV)

First Flight Magic

"An ecologist is someone who believes that a bird in the bush is worth two in the hand." I read that sentence recently and smiled at the aptness of it.

Ecology and conservation are subjects which in recent years have had much attention. Areas of green have disappeared under a ghastly covering of concrete. The habitats of small creatures have been in danger of destruction because of our thoughtlessness. The rape of our countryside in the name of progress has been stopped by those who care deeply about wildlife.

This year the blue tits returned to the nesting box outside the kitchen window. I wondered if they would come back because the box had been moved much nearer to the house in a garden-clearing operation. However, like loyal tourists, they returned to their favourite board residence and I was privileged to watch the whole process from nest reconstruction to the feeding of the young birds — a full-time occupation for Mum and Dad.

I was having breakfast when the first fledgling emerged to try an uneasy flight to the next tree. It climbed up the little thatch of the feeding box and sat for a moment or two contemplating the huge outside world.

I sat very still, not daring to move, for the little chap was only about four feet away from me. He shook out his sparse feathers and ventured on his flight. For me it was a magical moment. For him it must have been a terrifying experience.

We who live in Jersey, in the Channel Islands, are so fortunate for all around us is the beauty of coastline and countryside. We live close to nature and we learn much from it.

Robert Ingersoll, who died in 1899, wrote something which I think we all might remember:

In nature there are neither rewards nor punishments. There are only consequences.

Golden Daffodils

I hear much nowadays about extended families. What I have is an extended garden. There is the part which I own and cultivate. In addition to that there is, at this time of the year, an expanse of gold stretching down the valley which belongs to my friend, the daffodil grower.

His field of daffodils is the view from my kitchen window and, because the land slopes away, you get the impression that it is all part of my garden.

This year the field of gold has been a particular delight. As I stand at the kitchen sink, I feast my eyes on it and remember Gran of blessed memory.

My mother came to Jersey when she was 85 and died on the island just before she was 90. It could have been difficult transplanting such a well-established person from the north of Scotland to the most southerly of the Channel Islands. She was, however, a hardy plant and settled well into her new environment.

Her particular joy was the field of daffodils and she used to spend far too long standing at the kitchen sink admiring the view. Her fear that daffodils would become an unprofitable crop was very real and she dreaded the day when cauliflowers might take the place of her beloved golden crop.

As I too spend a long time at the sink, looking at the same flowers, I am constantly thankful that, so far, I have not become blasé about the many blessings I have. I am always surprised by the view from the window.

Only this week, for example, when I walked up to the shop for the morning paper, I noticed an absolute wealth of violets which were tucked into the bank. Somehow they have escaped the weedkillers which are such a tragedy for our wild flowers.

As I saw the violets and paused for a moment I uttered a prayer of thankfulness for eyes to see such beauty and a heart to rejoice in God who created all things.

Thank you for the ability to see, to love, and to be eternally grateful to You the Creator of our universe.

In Memoriam, Julius Caesar

In Memoriam:- Caesar C. Julius, soldier, statesman, lawyer, orator,

*man of letters, father of his country. Murdered in Rome, March 15,
44BC "the noblest man that ever lived."*

I cut out this *In Memoriam* notice from the *Times* because I
was intrigued by it. After all it is not often that an *In Memoriam*
notice is inserted in a newspaper over 2,000 years after someone's
death.

I remembered old Julius with a pang of affection for did I
not "do" Julius Caesar for School Certificate and as every pupil
knows that establishes a relationship which is enduring?

I wonder who inserted the notice in the Personal column.
There cannot be any surviving relatives! The only namesakes of
the noble Roman whom I can recall have been fierce dogs which
have strained at the end of great chains and have answered
reluctantly and with bad temper to the name of "Caesar."

There may I suppose be Julius Caesar societies which meet
together to bemoan the fact that their leader is dead and the
world will never see his like again. Perhaps Brutus, who dealt
the fatal blow which killed Caesar, left a bequest so that ever
after, a yearly notice might be placed in the *Forum* and the
Times inherited that!

On a more serious note, however, it is significant that Brutus
is remembered for the betrayal of Caesar and the words "Et tu
Brute", uttered by the dying Caesar, are symbolic of betrayal.

Judas Iscariot like Brutus is remembered for the betrayal of
his master. In the play Julius Caesar there is a memorable speech
which indicates that the good that we do is not so much remembered as the harm we have done. It is a sobering thought.

The evil that men do lives after them, the good is oft interred with their bones.

Befriend It!

I have a friend attached to a wall in a hotel in St Malo.

Let me explain.

After a delightful five days in France, I was attempting to sleep in a hotel bedroom in St Malo, conscious of the fact that it was necessary to get up at 6.30 French time, 5.30 our time to catch the ferry back to Jersey.

My sleep was frustrated by a pipe which was making the sort of noise which only French pipes can make in hotel bedrooms. I decided to inform the friend who was holidaying with me and who appeared to be asleep in the other bed unaware of my annoyance. The following dialogue took place.

Me: "I cannot sleep for that pipe"
Friend: "Befriend it."

I lay for a little while pondering the advice.

Me: "What exactly have you got in mind?"
Friend: "It is 11.30 and there is nothing that we can do about the pipe, so you must change your attitude to it. I suggest that you befriend it. Tell yourself that the pipe has a job to do. It meets with other pipes. It has an important task to do carrying the water round. It likes to make that little singing noise. It is a happy pipe and it is your friend."

I lay there in the darkness for a moment, shocked into silence. It had simply never occurred to me before to befriend a pipe. On the other hand of course one must learn to be adaptable.

I reflected that having a friend who is a psychologist as well as a friend who is a pipe makes me rich in friendship. In two minutes I was asleep.

God grant me serenity to accept things I cannot change, courage to change the things I can and wisdom to know the difference.

The Hosanna-hailer

"I'm Jesus" said the fair-haired prep schoolboy friend of mine.

We had been discussing the school Easter play and I was suitably impressed that he had been cast for such an important role.

"I know all the lines and I can be the narrator too, if you would like to hear them," he said confidently.

I expressed my pleasure at the thought of the one-man entertainment and prepared myself for the performance.

"You could come in with the Hosannas" he said generously. I nodded and tried to remember when the Palm Sunday crowd had offered their words of praise to the donkey-riding Jesus.

I was so intrigued listening to the young Jesus taking all the parts that I missed my cue and a pained look came over the face of the principal actor.

"I'm doing the Hosannas as well as everything else," he said in deeply injured tones. I looked suitably contrite and we went through it all again. When we finished, I apologised once again for my failure.

"It's all right," he said graciously "you can't expect Jesus to do everything, I have to remember to send for the donkey and . . ." his voice trailed off for he had been deflected by something he had seen in the garden outside.

As he left me rushing headlong out of the room, I thought that he had been right to reprimand me. He had asked me to do little enough as a "Hosanna-hailer." Like the Palm Sunday crowds, I had only to stand by and cheer but I had somehow missed my cue.

The crowds, who on Easter day shouted "Crucify, crucify" did not forget their lines. They needed no prompting. They came in "on cue."

Long after the conversation with my young friend had ended, the memory of our acting together remained. I had a picture in my mind of his pained expression when he uttered the words "You can't expect Jesus to do everything." Perhaps too often we expect just that.

He has no hands but our hands . . .

Tovey

"He looks rather like a rather long Scottie," said the girl at the end of the telephone.

"How much longer?" I said with that instant come-back which distinguishes the journalist from other civilized beings.

"Not very much longer," she said in a comforting voice.

When Tovey arrived to share my life, I could see that the description was half right. He looked very like a terrier from Scotland from the front, but from the back, he looked like something quite different.

He was also a good deal longer, and, from the outset, had none of the native dourness of some Aberdeen terriers.

Choosing a dog to share one's life is not easy. Had Tovey not been a stray with a chequered career, I might never have had the opportunity to acquire him.

His past is shrouded in mystery, but gradually glimpses of the life he has led have unfolded. Walking with him on his new lead through St Helier on the second day after his arrival, he passed all the shops without a second glance. Suddenly however he lifted his head and sniffed and then pulled me straight into a pub on the corner of Union Street.

Later that day, he sniffed and pulled me towards another establishment providing drink for the weary.

A stranger to the island, Tovey nevertheless recognized the familiar smell of the inn and I had to chuckle at his bad luck landing in the home of a well-known non-drinker.

Tovey is a stranger because there were no dogs in our Animal Shelter when I needed one. He came from another island but already he has wormed his way into my heart and into my life. I imagine he lived in the pubs of that other island because he found warmth and friendship there, and, no doubt, the odd potato crisp and sausage roll from a friendly innkeeper.

God gives us friends to make our journey lighter. He gives us dogs to make our journey merrier.

Your lucky Star

"When is Tovey's birthday?" a friend asked me.

I paused for a moment and wondered when the black dog with, as I often say, the Queen Anne feet was let loose on this world.

I often tell him that, if he were a piece of furniture, his feet would make him valuable. I do not in fact know his birthday for Tovey was born in Guernsey of unknown parentage. So nobody knows it!

Later that day someone asked me if I were a Capricorn or a Cancer. I thought for a moment or two and admitted to being a Sagittarian, but as I had never been interested in my horoscope it meant little to me. My friend was surprised by such lack of interest. "I would have guessed you were born under the sign of Sagittarius," she said knowingly.

I did not dare ask what particular weaknesses we Sagittarians display for I have many, though it would be nice to blame them on the moment at which I was born.

As Tovey is an orphan, so far as I know, but in any case I could not consult his mother about his natal day, I must assume that he was born under the Zodiacal sign of a free spirit.

I know how old I am but Tovey is ageless. It is possible to tell the age of a horse very accurately by looking at his teeth. Tovey has no upper teeth so he cannot be assessed in that way assuming, of course, that dogs are like horses in the matter of tooth age!

I have met people who are committed to the subject of astrology. They reckon that, within a second of birth, certain characteristics are part of our nature. I cannot argue against the concept with conviction for I have never studied the subject in any depth. I can argue the case from the Christian standpoint.

Whatever our nature, we can be changed by our belief in the Risen Christ. In the same way those of other faiths would claim that their life-styles are governed, not by the stars, but by their faith in God as revealed by their particular prophet.

In the hands of the Master Potter we can be changed to what he would have us be.

My Track-suit

I have for a long time wanted to possess a track-suit. Several stockists of these garments have welcomed me into their premises and allowed me to try on their wares.

My resemblance to Michelin Man has deterred me from purchasing a suit but now I have one. It is, for the record, blue with white piping.

My track-suit is borrowed but I was not loaned the garment to allow me to jog around the country lanes near my cottage. My desire for such a suit was inspired by a desire for indolence rather than a desire for keeping fit.

I had for long dreamed of long lazy winter evenings curled up by the fire with Tovey at my feet. The suit I had in mind would have resembled the cosy pyjamas of my childhood. The track suit does not resemble the lovely warm garments of yesteryear.

I hesitate to mention the reason why I am wearing the blue and white track suit. The truth of the matter is that I fell over a footstool in the dark and broke my shoulder! I had returned to the cottage and opened the front door to find the telephone was ringing. Not stopping to put the light on, I rushed to pick up the receiver. On the way I fell over the footstool and hit the side of the door. There was a crack like a pistol shot.

I must admit that the doctor, sister, staff nurse, radiologist and porters at our local Casualty Department were full of kindness. It was an eye-opener to see a Sunday night there. It was literally awash with patients, some drunk, some sober, but all of us in need of help.

They told me I had broken my Greater Tuberosity. I did not know I had one. Had I been asked about it, I would have thought it was a garden shrub.

So why the track suit? Well, it was the only garment which I could master with one hand. I am grateful to the friend from whom I borrowed it.

The breaking of the GT has taught me an important lesson. I must be more admiring of those with physical handicaps especially when they live such uncomplaining and useful lives.

I fear I have complained too much over my minor mishap.

I felt sorry for myself because I had no shoes and then I saw a man who had no feet.

Be Prepared!

"In the event of a nuclear fall-out I shall eat your tins of dog food and then I shall eat you," I said to Tovey as we sat together by a spluttering log fire.

Tovey wagged his tail hopefully. The mention of the word food had obviously struck a chord in his heart. The rest of the sentence passed him by — which was probably just as well as our relationship is fairly close.

I had just finished reading the instructions which had come with my newspaper about what to do in the event of a nuclear disaster when I had this particular conversation with Tovey. I have never been much good as a housewife who keeps large stocks of food for emergencies. It was only when I read the instructions that it occurred to me that I had not even replenished our minor stock of emergency rations since the cold weather. Then I had eaten my way through the last tin of beans.

The warning about contaminated rain water struck a further blow for, despite the assurances about the safety of the piped water supply, the provision of such a facility is not available to us in this primitive but delightful part of the Channel Islands.

"We had better lay in a stock of food and some bottled water." I said to Tovey who looked hopeful again.

I resolved to remedy the empty store cupboard situation and tried to think of all the items which I would feel I might enjoy when stranded in a nuclear fall-out situation.

I smiled as I thought of the effect the quite matter-of-fact government warning had had on me. I was not so much concerned about the fearfulness of the tragedy itself but on my own well-being. Nevertheless, the warning had struck home. Be prepared!

We all need warnings to shake us out of our apathy. Even so sometimes we ignore warnings — at our peril. A symptom ignored can sometimes result in an illness which has got a hold on us because of our failure to note the warning signal.

Sometimes too we ignore the voice of God, speaking through our conscience. We ignore that voice too at our peril.

Conscience is merely our own judgment of the right or wrong of our actions, and so can never be a safe guide unless enlightened by the word of God.

One Step is enough

Tovey's braking system failed during the recent bout of cold weather.

Tovey's feet, like the clock at Grantchester, are not only permanently showing the wrong time — ten minutes to three — but they have an obvious disadvantage in icy conditions.

This fact became obvious when we emerged from a two-day hibernation to see if we could walk to our village shop. I was devoid of provisions but I was in need of company and the local shop is where we, in our island paradise, go when we want news of our friends.

Before setting out on what appeared to be a minor glacier leading from the cottage to the top of the valley, I gave Tovey a lecture on his responsibility towards me. As he is no longer a free-range dog when we are out for walks but is permanently affixed to me by his lead, ascents such as that of the glacier have obvious dangers.

Walking at heel has never had much attraction for Tovey for he is by nature more of a husky-type dog. He would, if given half a chance, pull a sledge across Antarctica — well, that is what I believed until his braking system failed.

We set off up the hill and, within three feet of the front door of the cottage, when we had scarcely begun the ascent from base camp to the shop, Tovey went flat on his nose.

"It would obviously have been better for you if your feet had turned inwards," I said smugly. At that point my feet which neither turn inwards nor outwards slipped from beneath me and I sat down on the glacier.

I abandoned my trip to the shop and decided that I would have to do without the news bulletins which are such a vital link with our small outside world.

Two days later a friend lent me her boot chains, and these completely changed my life. I could walk with perfect safety and could, when the need arose, check Tovey's uncertain steps at critical moments on the glacier.

As I strode confidently up to the shop chain-booted, I found myself humming a line from a well-known hymn. There is a great deal of truth in Newman's "Lead Kindly Light" and the line which I hummed seemed particularly appropriate to me that day:-

Keep Thou my feet; I do not ask to see the distant scene; one step enough for me.

When Silence reigns

"If a man loses his voice it is a tragedy. If a woman loses her voice it is an act of God".

These words spoken to me many years ago by the man whom I loved and who shared my life, came back to me when I lost my voice totally for two days.

I had been suffering from a chest infection and thought that I was on the road to recovery when I awoke one morning and found that I could not utter a single word.

The complications which such a condition adds to the life of someone like me are enormous. I am a telephone addict and am, in no small way, responsible for the enormous profits which the Telecommunications Board have recently announced.

I also live with a dog who requires to hear me speak in order that he may be restrained from some mischief upon which he is frequently intent. Tovey's astonishment when he realised that I had lost my bark was total. He chased the neighbour's cat enthusiastically while I stood watching silently.

Realising that I was not in the business of social intercourse, I retreated to my typewriter and sat pounding away at the keys.

Neighbours who called found my silence had a strange effect on them. They all addressed me in sepulchral whispers for it is a strange fact of life that those who are stricken dumb are somehow infectious and the voices of others drop several decibels in their presence.

Towards the end of the second day I achieved a throaty whisper reminiscent of Marlene Dietrich in some smoke-filled night club. I ventured to sing "Falling in love again" but the effect was more macabre than alluring so I gave up the attempt.

On the third day I woke up and the first words that I uttered were "Get down!" These were delivered in stentorian tones to Tovey who was about to ascend the kitchen table legs. He leapt to the floor, realising sorrowfully, that the reign of terror had begun again and the silent days were over.

Now that I can speak again, I recall an old saying of my mother's which she was wont to write in autograph books:-

If your lips would guard from slips
Five things observe with care;
Of whom you speak, to whom you speak
And how and when and where.

Stay young in Heart

"Suddenly you look old" I said to Tovey when I glanced down to the spot where he was sitting in adoration at my feet. Tovey wagged his tail hopefully.

Old is not a word in his vocabulary nor is it a word that I would usually use to describe him. The powdering of white on his black coat gave him a distinguished air.

This sudden "air of distinction" was caused by his devotion to me while I was making pastry.

I am not the most careful of cooks, and the big pastryboard seldom catches all the flour which I liberally sprinkle on it. Tovey hopes for small pieces of uncooked pastry landing at his feet, and he had had a lucky morning. However, the flour sprinkled liberally on his coat had made him look much older. I gave him an extra piece of uncooked pastry because of his changed appearance.

Old age can creep upon us or overtake us quite rapidly. One moment we are young and skipping from rock to rock on the beach and the next moment we are behaving sedately, conscious that our physical energy is not what it once was.

It is important to have a young outlook. We must not let our brains harden as our muscles diminish.

How do we achieve this? By trying to accept change when it is good, and by standing firm for these values which are relevant in every age.

Lord keep me young in heart, even when the rest of me grows old.

Pray for Whisky

"Pray for whisky."

I stopped short in my tracks. As a preacher, I sometimes ask members of the congregation if they have specific requests for prayers. Children especially like to be involved in petitions and I usually ask the youngest members for whom I should pray publicly.

The request for whisky came from an angelic little boy kneeling with his friends around the communion rail. He did not look like an incipient alcoholic so I bent down to get further light on his particular request.

"Whisky's my cat," he whispered. I breathed a sigh of relief and could sense that the adults in the congregation could relax in their pews as the prayer unfolded.

On a recent visit to London, I spent some time in a telephone kiosk at Victoria station. Sitting outside were two people, a man and a woman, both of whom were in a pitiful state. I imagine they were meth drinkers. They were obviously at the end of their tether and a more tragic and pitiful sight it would have been hard to find.

Had I asked them at that moment what they wanted me to pray for I am sure they would have said another bottle of spirits to take away the grim reality of that morning of despair.

We all pray for the things which we most want and for the people whom we most love. Some pray to an unknown God and others to a familiar friend. For the Christian there is the certainty that all prayers are heard, although the answers are not always the ones we want to hear.

Christ, before his Crucifixion, gave us an example of praying for those whom we love, when He said to His disciples;-

"I pray for them; I am not praying for the world, but for those whom Thou hast given me, because they belong to Thee."

St John 17: verse 9 (NEB)

The closed Shop

I get a little irritated by shops which are not open when they should be. They display notices telling of their opening and closing times which are patently inaccurate. These shops usually belong to someone who is running their establishment single-handed. I have no doubt the temptation to slip out for a few moments is very great!

I recently wanted to buy something which I had seen in a shop which sells all manner of curious things. I noted that the shop would be open between the hours of 2 and 5 on a Tuesday. I made my way there and found it closed. I glanced at my watch which, like the clock at Grantchester, had its hands standing at ten to three.

Incidentally, discussing the Rupert Brooke poem in which he mentions the clock at Grantchester I discovered that the friend with whom I was discussing the matter had a quite different opinion on the poem than the one I held.

I had thought that the clock was remembered by the poet because its hands were permanently fixed at ten to three because it was broken. My more erudite friend told me that it was merely fixed in the mind of Rupert Brooke at ten to three.

To return to the closed shop!

I paced up and down for a while outside the shop and went away never to return. I had been misled by the notice and, in a fit of pique, decided not to buy the object of my desire.

It is always best to know where you stand with other people and with God. People are somewhat more unpredictable than God who never changes whatever the situation. He is the constant factor in our lives and he is always open to our needs.

I saw a rather apt notice which a barber in a Norfolk village displays. Perhaps it would be more appropriate for shops like the one which frustrated me recently.

This shop is closed all the week, unless it is open. Don't waste time waiting.

The Garage Squatters

I am not, by nature, a tidy person although I have, over the years, cultivated a certain orderliness in my life-style which makes for ease.

Strangely, I have always had an absolute obsession about having the garage tidy. For some reason, which may have been a pre-natal influence, the garage in chaos throws me into utter panic.

I have fought battles over the years with my nearest and dearest on the matter of keeping the garage tidy. In recent months I have to say that I have been fairly successful over my garage but suddenly a new factor has emerged. Someone has taken up residence in the place where I store my tools and my car.

I cannot inform the police because there is no way that one could describe my garage tenants as "sleeping rough." Indeed, at this moment I do not know where the couple are sleeping.

I have caught glimpses of them coming and going but where they are making their bed I know not. This means that I cannot tidy the garage — it is in urgent need of my attention — for I would be afraid that I might disturb my temporary residents.

Some three years ago two swallows moved into the garage and I had to wash the car roof every morning. My latest tenants have not so far discovered the joy of a car as a Portaloo! They are a pair of wrens and I have no idea in which corner they have built their nest.

I have therefore issued an edict against all garage tidying. We creep in and out getting tools, the lawn mower etc., as quietly as we can. I will leave my car outside soon for I imagine that the sound of the engine will cause baby wrens sleepless nights. Mothers, whether wren or human, know how wearying crying babies can be in the night watches.

I would like to see what the parents have chosen for their abode. The choice of building material is endless. The nooks and crannies are numerous and I wonder if the rugger boots which have hung on the nail for some years are housing a young family. I feel very privileged that they have chosen my garage for their home.

And entering into the field, he began to preach to the birds which were on the ground and suddenly all those on the trees came round and listened while St Francis preached and did not fly away until he had given them a blessing.
(Little Flowers of St Francis)

The Guide-man and his Dog

It was outside a church in Pontalier in Franche Comté that I saw the man standing patiently with the dog. The dog, a Doberman Pinscher, was wearing a harness. The man was obviously in his early twenties.

I did not know if they were waiting to cross the busy road or had an appointment to meet someone outside the church so I did not offer them help.

When I came out of the church, they were still there and I looked more closely at them. There was something odd about their relationship. Then I noticed something unusual. The *dog* was blind. The man was, in fact, the guide-man for the dog.

Later in the morning, I saw them again. They were threading their way through the tourist-crowded street and people stood aside to allow this unusual pair to pass. I think most of them would have assumed that it was a blind man with his guide-dog, not a blind dog with his guide-man.

When I return from any journey or holiday, I always have a host of memories stored up in my somewhat unreliable memory bank. I think the blind dog with his guide is one that I shall remember for a long time.

There were other scenes to remember from that French holiday but nearly all of them are memories of people and not places.

I shall remember the priest at a little village called Consolation who leaned out of his window to talk to us and show my friend and me his church. He suffered from heart trouble and, in the intense heat, he was a little breathless but he insisted on escorting us round his church. Afterwards he asked us if we would stay and share his lunch.

I will remember the little village of Consolation and that priest, I will remember the man and his dog for animals have a special place in my heart. I offer this prayer for animals:-

Hear our humble prayer O God for our friends the animals, Thy creatures. We pray especially for all that are suffering in any way, for the overworked and the underfed, the hunted, lost, or hungry, for all in captivity or ill treated and for those who must be put to death. We entreat for them Thy mercy and pity; and for those who deal with them we ask a heart of compassion, gentle hands and kindly words. In Christ's name, Amen.

Our Brother's Keeper

"Mother always used to get us children to crawl under the kitchen table and then she would sprinkle us with lovely holy water from Lourdes and we would all sit there until the thunder stopped."

I can still hear the voice of that Irish friend, who died tragically young, whenever there is a bad thunderstorm, as there was just recently, I remember how frightened she was during such a storm when I was with her.

The fear of the mother had communicated itself to the children, huddled under the kitchen table long ago. It had as a result become a lifetime phobia.

I was much more fortunate for I had a mother who rather

35

enjoyed thunderstorms, and I can remember her telling my brother and me to stay away from the windows during a violent bout of lightning while she sat looking out at it, enjoying the whole dramatic spectacle.

So much of our adult behaviour is programmed by our early life experiences. Children from secure happy homes have a head start in life over children whose early days are overshadowed by disruptions which range from constant arguments to actual violence.

There has been much publicity recently about children at risk in our society. They grow up with very little understanding of what love and caring mean in their young lives.

The sound of a key turning in a doorlock is not the prelude to a rush of young feet and happy shouts of "Dad." It is more likely to be the signal for children to run away and hide. Even the kitchen table is not a safe sanctuary for the battered child.

What can we do about the problem? We must be watchful and aware of our neighbours. We must remember that we are, indeed our brother's keeper.

We pray Father, for children everywhere especially for those who live in fear of those to whom they cannot turn for love.

Anti-ant Warfare

Many years ago I went to Sark for the very first time. It was in the month of May and I discovered a blue island.

I shall never forget the sight of those headlands, covered in bluebells, and the deeper blue sea below. I treasure the memory of my first glimpse of that little island.

This week I saw one bluebell but it was worth seeing. It had thrust itself up through the hard surface in a town street. It had cracked the surface of the recently laid road and thrust itself up as if to prove that men may lay roads but bluebells can destroy them.

Nature has a strange way of reminding us that we are not all-powerful. Take my ants, for example. Well, I wish someone *would* take them for they have decided that my cottage is more comfortable than their anthills. They have been everywhere for weeks. They have even invaded my bedroom and I have found their presence extremely irritating.

I have to admit that I find their persistence in the face of all ant deterrents very admirable. The arguments for unilateral disarmament have little sway with me. I did at first allow the ants to walk all over me in the mistaken belief that when they had explored every nook and cranny and taken intolerable liberties with my jam cupboard they would go away. I was wrong. They are here to stay. I have therefore armed myself to the teeth with powder, sticky jelly and sprays.

Talk not to me of passive resistance. The ants do not understand it! The ants are armed to the teeth. I am now an arsenal of anti-ant deterrents. I am slowly winning and I will triumph in the end!

Even as I write this, I hesitate. I recall the bluebell! It triumphed and one day, perhaps, ants will climb all over my derelict cottage when I am long dead. It is a sobering thought.

'As for man his days are as grass; as a flower of the field he flourisheth. For the wind passeth over it and it is gone; and the place thereof shall know it no more but the mercy of the Lord is from everlasting unto everlasting upon them that fear Him.'

Psalm 103; verses 15 — 17 (AV)

Do you like Butter?

Driving to the golf course early one Monday morning I saw a lovely, little tableau. I decided to brake in order to enjoy it.

It was a bright morning and there were two children going to school. They were wearing the royal blue uniform of their particular primary educational establishment and against the green background the contrast was very colourful. The children were flaxen-haired. Both were laughing uproariously.

The little boy had picked a buttercup and was holding it under the little girl's chin in the time-honoured manner. He had obviously been taught the ritual and knew that if the buttercup reflected under her chin then the answer to the question "do you like butter?" had got to be in the affirmative.

I was thrilled to see that in this day and age the old habit still continued. No doubt the day will come when the question will be "Do you like low-calorie hydrogenated vegetable oil with milk protein and acidity regulators?" In the meantime let us hope that butter wins the race for the sake of the buttercup!

The memory of that little scene remained with me throughout my round of golf and may even have contributed to my bad play!

There was an innocence about the children that transported me back to the buttercup ritual which I, too, was taught as a child.

I suppose most of us learned the buttercup trick at our mother's knee. That reminds me of an old adage;-

The good habits we learn at our mother's knee, the bad habits we pick up at other joints.

What do you do in the Winter?

I know it is approaching summer because the cherry trees flower and the men who do road work have taken their shirts off.

The trees looked a glorious delicate pink and so did the men's torsoes. I have already had my first tourist stopping to admire the clematis on the cottage and to ask me the sort of questions which tourists usually ask.

"What do you do here in the winter?," one very well-heeled lady asked in much the same way as early explorers must have asked aboriginal tribes how they spent their time. In the interests of our tourist campaign, I bit back the desire to say that we eat the holidaymakers, whom we kill and put in the deep freeze for the winter famine for asking silly questions. Instead I told her that we rather like winter-time. We all have different pastimes like flower clubs, debating, amateur dramatics and so on. I thought that made us sound rather civilized in the way they wanted us to be! My first Tourist went on up the hill contemplating no doubt our wide range of winter activities.

I was sent a poem recently which deals with encounters. I think it is relevant for all of us.

Only a smile in the crowded street

From the face of a friend you chance to meet

And yet it will brighten your life for days

And make you happy in countless ways

Only a word — a How-do-you-do

When griefs are many and friends are few

Will make you feel whatever befall

That life's worth living after all!

The hollow Tree

"Would you like to post mine as well?" I asked the small girl who had just finished posting a letter for her mother. She had been lifted up to place the letter in the slot because she was too small to reach.

Watching the joy on her face as she performed the simple task, I was transported back to my own childhood when I had performed a similar task with great pleasure.

In time I, too, lifted up a small boy to post letters in the pillar box at the end of our road. I can remember the slight feeling of disappointment when he told me that he could now reach the box himself by standing on tiptoe.

In my own childhood, there was a hollow tree near to where we had a summer cottage. The cottage did not belong to us but we rented it each year and the owners moved into what was called "the bothy" in the garden.

I imagine they lived in great discomfort. My mother used to tell me that the two months at the cottage were a time of testing for her.

I recall the twin-burning paraffin stove on which she had to cook. I have no doubt that she longed to get back to our city home where the cooking facilities, and every other facility, were more sophisticated. She endured the annual sojourn of discomfort because it was supposed to be good for my brother and for me to breathe good country air.

It is strange how the sight of that child posting the letter sparked off in my mind memories of my childhood. I could remember the excitement of finding a letter in the hollow tree. I could feel for a moment arms round my waist and the joy of being lifted up to post a letter although it was so many years ago.

Help us Father, to teach and show children the beauty of your world. Help us to lift them up to see your Love and your care for them.

Slow me down, Lord

The Boilery in the cottage is the room where the central heating boiler lives. I have to go through the Boilery on the way to the garage and I have a poster affixed to the Boilery door which tells me to slow down.

The poster depicts a covered bridge of the type still to be seen in New England and has an instruction above the bridge for those who intend to cross. It says simply "*Walk* across this bridge."

Cardinal Cushing wrote a well-known prayer on the subject of slowing down and the words on the poster are a reminder to me of the need to make haste slowly.

I have recently acquired another poster which I have hung up beside the "Slow me Down, Lord" one. This new poster is entitled "Whose Job Is It?" The artist has chosen three handsome cocks to discuss the subject of job allocation.

I have not yet worked out why the designer chose to illustrate the text with these handsome cocks, for they do not appear to me to have any relevance to the message. However the message itself is so true that I can commend it to people in many walks of life.

One of the difficulties which everyone experiences when doing voluntary work is getting people to take on a particular task. The annual general meeting of nearly every association to which I have ever belonged is usually sparsely attended. There is a general fear that attending the AGM may well land one in a position which will lead to extra work.

Asking for volunteers to run a fund-raising effort, for example can be a thankless task. People become adept at offering excuses for resisting such opportunities. I do not know if the writer of my new poster had such people in mind or could it simply be that this was a family story? So often in a family everyone expects that someone else will do the job. In the end no one does it.

This is a story about four people named 'Everybody' 'Somebody' 'Anybody' and 'Nobody'. There was an important job to be done and Everybody was asked to do it. Everybody was sure Somebody would do it; Anybody could have done it but Nobody did it. Somebody got very angry about that, because it was Everybody's job. Everybody thought Anybody could do it but Nobody realized that Everybody wouldn't do it. It ended up that Everybody blamed Somebody when Nobody did what Anybody could have done.

The Painter

I painted the porch last Saturday. Although this may not seem to be an earth-shattering event or even one worthy of comment in a world which is fraught with so many larger events and issues, I wish to announce it to the world at large.

Painting is not one of my accomplishments. I first took it up (I mean house-painting, not the more artistic type which artists practise) many years ago in Malta. It was in September when the Maltese weather can be unbearably hot and humid and it all began in the middle of the night when I could not sleep. I got up having decided to paint the wardrobe white. I had been thinking about doing it for some time and I was merely waiting for the moment of inspiration to come. At three in the morning I began my task.

While I could not honestly compare the painting of the wardrobe to the work on the ceiling of the Sistine Chapel, which Michelangelo undertook, I did my best. Unfortunately I was wearing at the time a black nightdress. When I had finished the wardrobe, I decided to join up the spots of paint on the nightdress. The effect of the joined-up blobs was vaguely surrealist and neither the wardrobe nor the nightdress looked much better for my ministrations.

I consequently put aside the painter's brushes and it was not until much later that I took them up again.

I found that I had not lost my old touch. The porch looked only slightly better and, as I was having the floor tiled anyway, (it was just as well as a blue floor with white spots looks odd) all was not lost!

For all do-it-yourself experts, may I suggest this little motto:-

Experience is still the best teacher. An added advantage is that you get individual instruction.

The Grass is always greener. . .

She was standing in the middle of a narrow part of the road as I came round the corner. I skidded to a standstill and was glad to find that my brakes were reliable. She stood sorrowfully with the chain, a symbol of agricultural restrictive practices, dangling from her head. The high grass verge which bordered the field from which she had escaped must have proved a difficult descent and the field, on the opposite side of the road which had attracted her attention, was inaccessible.

I was faced with the problem of getting one reluctant Jersey cow back into her field. Of course I could have left her in the middle of the road but another car might have rounded the corner even more speedily than I did. My heart softened as I imagined the accident that might take place. A car here or

45

there in the island might not be missed but good cows are valuable.

Normally I would have tackled my task with resolution but I was not dressed for the task. There is something incongruous about leading a cow when one is dressed for a tea-party. However, "nothing venture, nothing win" I murmured somewhat inanely and, grasping the chain firmly, mounted the bank.

It was at this point that I realized that my rescue act was being hindered by my friend the cow. She preferred the dangers of the road to the boredom of the field and a tussle ensued. Then, perversely but with characteristic feminine change of mind, she suddenly decided to co-operate. The resultant lack of tension on the chain as I was half-way up the slope would have made a good shot for a slap-stick comedy film.

The next stage of the operation was easily accomplished and if the farmer, who found two of his cows tied together, was puzzled, I can assure him that, not having a mallet and stake handy, this was the only solution. Our method of tethering cows to a stake in the ground by a chain is only possible if a mallet is to hand!

The grass often appears to be greener in the next field. Human beings and animals share this delusion. It is only when we achieve the philosophy of a man like the Apostle Paul that we are able to say with him:-

For I have learned in whatever state I am therein to be content.
Philippians 4, verse 11 (AV)

Help us to laugh

When I was last in California, I bought several postcards which had terse messages printed on them.

My favourite one has just fallen out of a pigeon hole in my desk. It is decorated with a dragon breathing out fire and these words are written in black on a pea-green background.

"Don't be afraid to hurt my feelings; all you risk is my unbounded rage."

When I saw the card in a shop in San Francisco, I felt that I had to buy it for it summed up an attitude of mind which criticism sometimes produces in me. I have to struggle hard to accept criticism gracefully.

Sometimes I lose the struggle and the result is that my feelings get hurt and I feel rage welling up within me.

I envy these fortunate people who do not feel passionately about things. I admire people who remain calm when everything is falling around them.

I am not a calm, self-controlled person by nature. I have to struggle to maintain my temper and, I must confess, I have been known to vent my anger on inanimate objects.

The lawnmower has suffered from many a kick when it refuses to start and my aching toes merely remind me of the lack of self-control which the lawnmower brings out in me.

"You should count up to ten", my mother used to say when she saw the storm-clouds gathering. Alas, ten never provided a long enough gap for me to stifle my temper, and I have reached two hundred on some occasions when faced with those who refuse to acknowledge their own stupidity or who have hurt my feelings.

I think one should probably learn to laugh at oneself in order to conquer oneself. There is a prayer by A. G. Bullivant which has something of this in mind:—

Give us a sense of humour Lord and also things to laugh about
Give us the grace to take a joke against ourselves and to see
the funny side of things we do
Save us from annoyance and bad temper, resentfulness against
our friends
Help us to laugh even in the face of trouble
Fill our minds with the love of Jesus. Amen.

from The One Who Listens by Etta Gullick and Michael Hollins
published by Hodder and Stoughton

O taste and see

"You cannot possibly know what it tastes like until you have tried it," a mother said to a small boy sitting opposite to me in a crowded restaurant.

"I know what it tastes like," said the small boy stubbornly. "I can *see* what it tastes like."

The mother looked across at me, trying to hide a smile. The little boy had won that particular battle with the illogicality of the child defeating the logical adult. He knew what it tasted like because he could *see* it. His imagination was sufficient guide.

As I carried on eating and, at the same time, doing the crossword puzzle, I found myself thinking that we often refuse to be adventurous because we have preconceived ideas of what something will be like.

It is said that the man who ate the first oyster deserved a medal for bravery. Oyster lovers who have followed the same slimy track would agree!

It could be argued that being unadventurous is a fault of the middle-aged and the elderly, but, in my experience, I have found the young curiously hide-bound in their ideas.

The child who was sitting opposite to me was running true to type and there would be many years of fish and chips before the avocado pear and the gourmet meal would be tried.

It is not only in food that we lack the spirit of adventure for we are curiously inhibited in many other ways.

I recently met a man whom I have known well by sight for years. He had dyed his hair and had a very obvious bubble perm. I looked at him in astonishment but admired his daring.

I often meet people who tell me that they sometimes consider the values of Christianity but never risk discussing them or going to Church to learn more about the Christian way of life. Some of them suspect that the demands made upon them would be greater than they would be prepared to make and so they do not give it a trial.

G. K. Chesterton wrote:—

It is not that Christianity has been tried and found wanting. It has been tried and found difficult.

Linoleum

I did not know until recently how linoleum came into being. I did not even know that it got its name from two Latin words, *linum* and *oleum* which mean respectively flax and oil.

It is 101 years since Frederick Walton, the son of a Yorkshire engineer, noticed that a skin of dry oil had formed on a tin of paint which had been left with its lid off.

He wondered how he could make use of the skin and his inventive brain eventually came up with the product which soon covered the floors of factories and homes.

His floor-covering composition was made by mixing oxidised oil with ground up cork. His product was complete when he thought of rolling out his composition on a canvas backing.

When I read the account I found myself transported in imagination back to the shiny linoleum floor of the kitchen of my childhood home. The floor was so well polished that the pattern had gone but it glowed in the reflection of the black kitchen range and no one ever thought of replacing it with a new floor covering. In those far-off days no one thought that the kitchen was a room on which one should spend a small fortune in expensive furnishings!

As I recalled that old linoleum, and thought of my new-found knowledge about the way the product is made, I realised afresh that great inventions and innovations are so often the result of someone looking at a situation from a new angle. Countless people had seen the skin on a tin of unlidded paint before Walton saw it. He worked out what could be done with the skin.

It was said that it was the mould growing on a piece of wedding cake that gave Sir Alexander Fleming a lead on his search for penicillin.

It was the sight of a kettle lifting the lid with the force of steam that gave Stephenson the idea of harnessing the steam of motivation.

Great ideas often spring from commonplace happenings.
Great examples are given by ordinary lives gloriously lived.

Gone for a Burton

Nothing dates us more than the slang we use. Those of us who lived through the 1939-45 war have expressions which are incomprehensible to newer generations.

Obviously we have eliminated some of the expressions which were once our current verbal coinage but others linger on. We may know that to "crash our swedes" was once the expression used for having a nap, but "Harry Crashers", which became a development of that, has ceased to be used as have so many other Harry expressions.

One of the well-thumbed books on my shelves is *Brewer's Dictionary of Phrase and Fable*. Leafing through it, I came across the meaning of the phrase "gone for a Burton." It was a term in daily use in the Services. A person who had "gone for a Burton" was usually missing, presumed killed.

Brewer suggests that Burton was a place associated with beer and drink. To say that someone had "gone for a Burton" meant they had gone for a drink. In wartime "the drink" became

51

synonymous with the sea. So a pilot shot down over the sea was described as having "gone for a Burton."

There has always been a tendency to disguise "death" in all sorts of terms. We speak of "the departed" in hushed tones. We speak of those who have "gone beyond", those who have "passed over". We try to disguise the fact that someone has *died* because death is simply not acceptable.

Yet if there is one thing which the Christian should rejoice in it is the fact that Christ conquered death for all time.

At Easter we sing a hymn which proclaims the fact that Christ died "to make us good". If we believe He died to conquer death, then we must not view death as an unwelcome guest but as a friend who rids us of the limitations of this earthly body.

I do not fear death; I fear living without hope of life after death.

It's never too late to apologise

Nearly fifty years after the *New York Times* had written a certain story, the editor of that great newspaper printed an apology in connection with it. As it concerned the possibility of space research, I filed it away and brought it out this week.

On January 13, 1920, the newspaper had scoffed at Professor Goddard, the father of space research, for his belief that a rocket could function in a vacuum. "The professor seems to lack only the knowledge ladled out daily in high schools," the newspaper stated scathingly. In 1969, as Apollo XI hurtled towards the moon, the *New York Times* decided: 'It is now definitely established that a rocket can function in a vacuum. *The Times* regrets its error."

It took a long time for Professor Goddard's theory to be established. In 1920 it must have seemed incredible that a rocket could function in a vacuum, but Goddard was very much ahead of his time.

It is never too late to apologise.

This prayer is for those who communicate either through the written or spoken word. It may also be helpful to people like me who sometimes express ill-thought-out opinions in too facile a way.

We ask thy forgiveness for anything which has marred our day; for any word which now we wish we had not spoken; for any sentence which now we wish we had never written; for any deed which we now wish we had never done; for everything which makes us ashamed when we remember it.

Relationships

"I don't actually like him," said the woman to her friend in the supermarket. "I mean it is better working for someone you like, isn't it?"

Her friend was deflected for a moment as she chose some bacon. There was a pause. "You don't have to like him, he pays you doesn't he?" she said sensibly.

I am not, by nature, an eavesdropper but as people are my principal interest, I do enjoy hearing exchanges of view which total strangers occasionally allow me to hear.

In this instance the strangers were about forty years old and I would imagine they both worked in offices. They had probably always worked except for a short period when the children were young and they needed to be at home. After the children had gone to school, they had returned to work and were both wage-earners and homemakers.

It is a fairly common pattern for many people and I have always admired those who hold down responsible jobs and are competent home-makers. I use the word home-maker advisedly for it is not quite the same thing as housewife. To make a home a happy place for one's family takes a very special sort of expertise.

As the two ladies moved away from the bacon counter still engrossed in conversation, I found that I was pondering the dilemma which faced the one unhappy in her job.

Many people have to struggle with difficult relationships. Some find their marriages are at breaking-point. Some find their teen-age children have grown away from them. Others find in-laws impossible and there are, of course, those who find the people with whom they work hard to endure. Is there a solution?

Perhaps we have to start with ourselves and see if there is anything in us which makes relationship difficult.

Self-examination is not easy. As someone has said;

What we see depends mainly on what we look for.

Bad Listeners

I was intrigued when I heard a naturalist talking on the radio about how kangaroos got their name. Apparently "kangaroo" is Australian aboriginal language for "What did you say?"

The naturalist told of an early Australian settler who was with an aboriginal when a great animal with a baby in a pouch jumped past them. "What's that?" the astonished settler asked. "Kangaroo" said the aboriginal who was somewhat hard of hearing. From that time on, according to this naturalist, the animals which have such an endearing way of jumping and which have built-in carrycots have been called "kangaroos."

I do hope the naturalist was not pulling our collective legs. I want to believe his account and I have not risked looking up any reference books in case I am disillusioned! I would, therefore, be grateful if readers fluent in Australian aboriginal dialect, would refrain from writing.

"What did you say?" is a phrase we all use when we fail to catch something said to us. We may be hard of hearing or we may be simply paying scant attention to the speaker. To be a good listener is, however, an art which can be cultivated. So often we are so engrossed in our own thoughts, or longing to get our own word in, that we fail to listen.

People occasionally wonder if God hears their prayers because their petitions are not answered in the way they would like them to be. God hears all our prayers but we sometimes fail to listen to His reply.

Make me a good listener, Lord, so that I
can hear what you are saying to me

Good Intentions

I am now the proud possessor of a loft ladder, so I have a loft and I have a ladder. I do not unfortunately have one of those devices that work on a hinged trapdoor and, which, when pulled, reveal a staircase which descends from the loft.

I have been considering buying a loft ladder to help with my forays into the loft for some years. My steps which nearly reach to the ceiling are, alas, fraught with danger.

To begin with the trapdoor has to be lifted out. To get the trapdoor out of the hole is the first difficult part of the operation and I am frequently hit on the head in the attempt. Then I have to descend the step-ladder carrying the trap-door!

Swaying on top of the stepladder, seeing stars, is good neither for deportment nor balance. I can still recall one fearsome occasion when stepladder, trapdoor and yours truly landed on the floor simultaneously.

You may well be wondering what prevents me from having the trapdoor adapted to include a folding loft ladder. There is a difficulty however here. It could not be hinged properly. I rather feel I must endure the present situation for ever.

I hope not to look down one day from the celestial regions and see my obituary with the words "Suddenly as the result of a hit on the head with a trapdoor . . . "

The loft ladder is like so many other things that are improvements I intend to make, but which I put off doing because of my inability to work out how they could be achieved.

In life some are like me born putters-off. We know that something should be done but we do not get on with it. They say the path to hell is paved with good intentions. I, for one, know it to be true.

O God let me not put off making decisions, and doing that which I should do. Help me to be resolute in my life just as your Son was resolute in His when He died for me.

Pain

I know that pain is a symptom of disease so to remove the pain may not benefit the sufferer. I do however have to admit that if I were given one special gift, it would be the ability to take away pain from those people who have to endure it as a daily portion of their lives.

Pain can be caused in so many ways. Naturally we associate it with illness and disease. Dis-ease, as opposed to ease, is exactly what the name implies. The lack of ease means a daily struggle to find a way of coping with grinding and perpetual pain.

I know that many pains can be controlled by modern drugs. But not all pains are so controlled. Some friends of mine endure the long pain of the arthritis which makes their daily living a constant struggle.

There are others whom I know who suffer from the pain of loss. The person they loved most in the world has died and they cannot come to terms with their bereavement. I have tried to help them find relief from this particular burden but know that, in the end, they will have to find the way through the pain on their own.

Others whom I know have suffered from the pain of desertion. the person they most loved has walked out and found someone else to love. The pain of rejection is very hard to bear. At least the bereaved person was not rejected.

Each loss is different. It is no good offering the same comfort to the one whom death has robbed of companionship as you do to one who has been abandoned in favour of another.

Pain is no respecter of persons. In most lives some anguish comes unexpectedly and the shadows fall across our pathway and darken the sunlight. We cannot see how the day will ever be bright again. Gritting one's teeth and endeavouring to ignore the agony is one way. Praying for strength is another.

Amy Carmichael was a missionary who was bedridden for years. She wrote many wise words to comfort those who suffered as she did. I like her prayer for strength:—

Before the winds that blow do cease
Teach me to dwell with thy calm.
Before the pain has passed in peace,
Give me my God to sing a psalm.
Let me not lose the chance to prove
The fulness of enabling love.
O love of God do this for me
Maintain a constant victory.

from Love is my meaning, edited by Elizabeth Barratt,
published by Darton, Longman and Todd.

The throw-away Society

I have discovered a new talent. I have become a mender of deck chairs.

This latent talent was aroused in me when I found two friends who were intent on throwing out expensive chairs which only needed some repairs to be carried out on them.

Chairs for the garden seem to have a specially built-in obsolescence nowadays. They do not resemble the teak deck-chair which I gave away in 1972 when we sold our family home in Aberdeen.

The chair was a present to my mother in 1913 in Malaya and it was in constant use until 1972. Oh, yes, the canvas had been renewed. It never occurred to us to think that you did not replace it at regular intervals. It never entered our collective minds that the chair was no longer usable. The frame was as good as new — as my mother frequently remarked. She had lain on it both on the outward journey to the Far East, back again and every summer since.

Today's lightweight chairs are much easier to move around the garden but they are inclined to be unsatisfactory in all sorts of ways. Some have canvas with a built-in short life. Others have frames which rust at the first gentle drop of summer rain.

The ones I mended needed new strapping. I have also mended one double chair with loose cushions, two single chairs of the same kind and now I am about to embark upon a whole series of small chairs which need new canvas. I am not in the market for orders but I am distinctly swollen-headed about my new talent.

We live in a throw-away society. Not only do we readily discard possessions which could be repaired and renovated, but we have thrown overboard standards which once we held dear.

I think we should be conservationists not only of the countryside and our heritage but also of the moral fabric of our society
which is in constant danger of being thrown down.

It is not guided missiles
but guided morals that are our great need today.

G. L. Ford

The Fear of Silence

I find that there is a new fear abroad in the world — a fear of
silence.

People go to extraordinary lengths to escape this fear. Some
leave the television on from early morning to late at night so
that it becomes like wallpaper, part of the decor. It is part of
the furnishings in a room and one is only vaguely aware of it.

It is a noise and a picture coming from a box in the living-room.
Many people do not paper only the living-room with television.
The kitchen and the bedrooms are similarly decorated.

Others seek to escape from silence by maintaining incessant
contact with a transistorised radio with earphones, through which
a constant diet of music surges.

Walking along a country lane, travelling in a bus or train, I
constantly notice this phenomenon namely, people with intent
faces shutting out the world around them as they listen to the
sound transmitted to them through the tiny receiver which they
are carrying.

Some listen to classical music. Some are intent upon current affairs talk. Others are listening to the sort of music which is their escape from reality.

The other day I saw a young mother pushing a child along a country road. The mother was oblivious to the child's chatter for she had her transistor ear plugs firmly in place. What gems she must have been missing!

It is both the desire to escape from reality and the fear of silence which I find alarming. In the silence God speaks through the song of a bird or through the sighing of the wind in the trees. He can speak through the roar of the waves breaking on the shore or in the murmur of bees on a hot sunny day. He can certainly speak through the voice of a little child.

If we insulate ourselves against the sounds of the natural world, we cease to enjoy the stillness of just listening. We may even lose the opportunity of charging our batteries from God's power-house of love.

Be still and know that I am God.

Psalm 46, verse 10
(NIV)

Beauty Contests

I occasionally get into trouble for expressing my disapproval of beauty contests. I am totally opposed to them and never hesitate to say so, publicly and privately. I do not even like "Beautiful Baby" competitions because every mother, except the one whose baby wins the contest, feels aggrieved.

When it comes to adult contests, I find they engender a good deal of sadness and animosity among the contestants in the big commercial events.

I have been accused of being narrow-minded on the subject and told that it was because the girls were scantily dressed that I disapproved. My critics were wrong. I think that if one is judging all the points of the female form as if they were cattle, the girls would be better nude!

Beauty contests have indeed been likened to cattle shows but in this they do the organisers of such shows an injustice. After all cattle shows are held because it is important for the breeders to see the line from which their cattle are being bred. The class for the "best uddered cow" at the cattle show always makes me chuckle.

I have had fierce arguments with men about the morality of "Miss World" contests and about the entertainment value of such shows when they are televised. I am usually accused of sheer jealousy because I would have a greater chance of running a three-minute mile than of winning such a contest! To know one's limitations is, is it not, half the battle of life!

The book of Proverbs is full of admonitions for men who are fooled by thinking that a woman's outward appearance is a clue to her inner nature:-

Charm is deceptive, and beauty is fleeting, but a woman who fears the Lord is to be praised.

Proverbs 31, verse 30
(NIV)

A Victorian Blessing

Some years ago a friend gave me a Victorian paper picture. It is difficult to know how to describe the charm of the little paper triptych except to say that it is divided into three panels, the middle one of which has a silk background with a blessing written on it.

Round the blessing is a garland of paper flowers of the type which decorated Victorian scraps of that period. The outer panels are decorated like doilies of the kind which no proud housewife would have dreamed of being without.

Crocheted doilies like linen doilies were used on plates when one served cakes for tea. The material doilies gave way to paper ones. The little triptych now in my possession always reminds me of the tea parties of old when cake-stands with plates of fattening delights were part of the afternoon tea scene. The plates invariably had paper doilies ensuring that the mouth-watering eclairs and meringues were elegantly displayed.

This little Victorian memento sits on my old music cabinet which serves as a dressing-table. They are both from the same period and give me pleasure.

Old things are important to me for they recall an age of crafts-manship which has virtually if not totally disappeared. The inlaid work on the music cabinet is worn with many years of polishing, but it is a witness to a skill which has lost its popularity so far as today's furniture-making is concerned.

Fashions in clothes and furniture change but certain aspects of beauty do remain. The importance of line and detail of finish, are the marks of a good product, whatever the period.

When I was dusting the cabinet the other day, the little triptych fell down. As I replaced it, I read the blessing which, like so much that is worthwhile, has stood the test of time. Surrounded by its tiny wreath of flowers, this is what the Victorian maker of the memento wrote:-

May the blessing of God attend thee, and the sun of Glory shine unceasingly around thy paths. May no sorrow dim the brightness of thy days or disturb thy peaceful slumbers, and when the length of years makes thee tired of earthly pleasures, and the curtain of death closes around thy last moments, may the angels of God attend thee, so that the lamp of life shall not receive one rude blast to hasten its extinction.

Do-gooders?

"You only do things for other people because it gives you a kick," a young cynic said to me not very long ago.

I can remember stopping in my tracks and looking at him. He was angry with society, fed-up with me, disillusioned with life and he was only 20 years old.

He was determined to get me to lose my temper and at that moment he nearly succeeded. However, I took a deep breath and told him that there might be some truth in what he was saying for helping other people does indeed give the helper a feeling of satisfaction. It does of course, at the same time, make the person helped feel at a disadvantage.

"Go on, give me one good reason for doing something for someone else for nothing" went on my tormentor. I paused and chose my words carefully.

"There is no reason other than the fact that love is the force which persuades us to do something which is sometimes difficult, time-consuming and often boring," I said gently. "For example I ought not to be sitting talking to you for I have a great deal to do, but you have asked for my opinion about your life-style so because I love you, I have to give my time and my concentration and at the same time keep my temper which, quite frankly, I am finding it very difficult to do."

He looked taken aback for a moment then spat the word "love" in the sort of tone which devalued it instantly.

"Love suffereth long and is kind," I said to him gently, "and the only reason for many people giving up a great deal of time to all sorts of organisations, societies and clubs is, first, because they may enjoy doing the work and secondly, because they have a concern for their fellow-men and women which is inspired basically by love.

At this point he burst into a guffaw of mirth and went into a tirade about "do-gooders." I could see that I was not reaching him at all and we parted — regretfully on my side but with unbounded relief on his part.

William Temple wrote a prayer about love which has a sentence which applies to my young friend and to others like him.

O God of love, we pray Thee give us love;
Love of those with whom we find it hard to bear.
And love of those who find it hard to bear with us.

Third Time unlucky

I took to nicotine like a duck to water at a very young age.

My brother, who was two years my senior, caught me smoking

when I was ten years old. I had found his secret supply! His threat to tell "them" had the desired effect and I refrained from becoming a habitual smoker until I was in my late teens.

I then became a very heavy smoker and it took me another ten years to beat the habit. That is a long time ago but for those people who tell others that, after a few weeks of abstinence, the craving will cease, I can assure you that that was not true for me. Indeed, there are times today when in moments of crisis, I feel I would welcome a cigarette.

My father and I shared many a cigarette together for we were close friends, but he would never allow me to take the third light from a match.

"It's unlucky," he would say, blowing out the match and striking a fresh one.

It was many years later that I discovered the origin of that superstition. Apparently in the trenches in the 1914-18 war a soldier could risk taking the second light but if a match was kept alight for a third smoker, there was the danger of the enemy seeing the flickering light and the bombardment would begin.

I thought of my battle with nicotine when I read recently of the fearful statistics which reflect society's problems with the drug addict and the alcoholic. They need prayers and they need help.

In a book called *"Prayers for Pagans"* there is a poignant passage;

He staggered down the steps and fell, Lord, a crumpled mass on the footpath. His bottle broke and liquid spilled across the walk.

"He's drunk" I thought — disgust, disdain. Until . . . two girls rushed from a nearby car and cried:

"It's Daddy. Please help. He's ill."

Smile!

I have a sense of humour which has stood me in good stead down the years. I am more liable to laugh than I am prone to weep. Indeed there have been times when I have been faced with the choice and have opted for laughter because crying never seems to achieve much. It can possibly attract sympathy, but sympathy can be a weakening commodity.

I can remember my mother telling me that she had fallen rather painfully when she was alone at home. "There didn't seem to be much point in crying," she said philosophically, "there was no one about to hear."

I am not referring of course to the depressives of the world when I write in this light-hearted way. I am more than conscious of the plight of those who suffer from such an agonising mental illness and one which cuts them off from society.

The depressive lives in a grey valley where light does not penetrate. With the aid of drugs or even more drastic intervention, the plight of the depressive can be made bearable, but his/her lot is a hard one. We do well to remember all those whom we know who suffer from such diseases when we say our prayers.

But back to the things which make me laugh.

I found a quotation recently from Jerry Lewis. I wondered when I read it if I could use it to end one of these Saturday Specials. It has no Christian or moral basis but it does illustrate a great truth nevertheless. What it does is demonstrate that a sentence or a request can mean something wholly different from the original meaning of the words.

Jerry Lewis' father must have had a wonderful sense of humour for this was Jerry's story.

When I was a kid I said to my father. "Daddy will you take me to the zoo?" He answered "If the zoo wants you, they can come and fetch you."

Sometimes we have to listen carefully then weigh our answers, especially if the questioner really needs a considered reply.

A Power Failure

As I was writing this, there was a power cut. I know because I am the owner of an electronic typewriter.

I do not want to boast about this piece of good fortune for it is a new acquisition. It is therefore tempting to mention it "in passing." I have in fact dragged it into conversation several times.

The electronic typewriter has a limited built-in memory — but so have I. It also erases errors. It has not however got a built-in dictionary, a facility which a word processor owned by friends does possess.

I drop their word processor into the conversation too when I am trying to impress people with the fact that I have friends who have such a treasure in their study.

At this moment (to revert to the power failure) my electronic typewriter, with its memory and fancy eraser, is silent and useless. In a power cut such a machine is indeed more useless than a slate and pencil. I did not think when I bought it that power-cuts were going to be regular occurrences. (If that is a slight exaggeration, it is just that I am apt to exaggerate when I am frustrated).

I waited ten minutes before getting Old Faithful out of the cupboard. Old Faithful, you see, is powered by me and is not dependent on some foreign power. I depress the keys and Old Faithful obeys my every whim.

We all depend on the services of other people. We also depend on God for our ultimate well-being, for he is the source of power. But with him, there are no power failures.

My grace is sufficient for you.
My power is made perfect in weakness.

2 Corinthians, 12, verse 9 (NIV)

My Appointment

"He might be able to fit you in but he is very busy at the

moment. Perhaps you could phone again at lunch-time when he could look up his diary."

The voice at the other end was very non-committal and I spent an anxious morning wondering if I would, in fact, get an appointment.

It was not exactly a matter of life and death but it was nevertheless essential that I should be fitted in if possible. I tried to convince myself that old clients, or should I say patients, ought to have a priority but in other days, his diary was not fully booked. Then he was glad to have me telephone and was only too happy to fit me in. However, like all busy and hardworking men, he had found his time more taken up and his diary had become completely filled.

The morning passed slowly and I was glad that it was time to dial his number again. Somewhat hesitatingly I gave my name and, in a slightly ingratiating way, asked for an appointment. There was an audible sigh which came right down the telephone and into my ear but then came the reassuring words: "I have a cancellation at 10.30 next Thursday. I could fit you in then." He cut off my thanks and added: "I hope it won't be as bad as last time." I hung up hastily lest he changed his mind and I went off to make a note of the day and time in my own diary.

I also hoped, for his sake, that it would not be as bad as last time. If I have given the impression that I had made a dental appointment or a doctor's appointment, I hasten to say that it is the chimney sweep who is coming next Thursday! His parting remark about the condition of the chimney last year did not go unnoticed. He had waxed eloquent on the condition of our chimney and on the amount of soot which we had managed to collect.

All chimneys are different, he told me, and our chimney was particularly awkward.

71

I suppose that, as with people, chimneys differ, but as soot spoils any chimney from drawing, so sin spoils every life.

May the love of God sweep through our lives and leave us refreshed.

Hedgehogs in Conversation

My camera never has a film in it when a subject presents itself that if captured at the critical moment, would make photographic history.

Tovey was outside the house inspecting the security fence and gate which I have installed to keep him at home—at some expense.

Once a free-range dog, Tovey now finds his activities somewhat limited.

I took no notice at first of his barking. However, when the noise continued, I went out to see what had aroused his displeasure.

Outside the smart gate which a friend called David had made for us, there was a lovely sight—two hedgehogs standing nose to nose—either in deep conversation or in silent adoration.

Safe behind the gate, they remained immobile, even when I leaned over to speak to them. On a bright moonlit night, the picture they made, wrapped as they were in hedgehog conversation, was enchanting.

I decided to capture the moment for posterity, went inside, took out my camera and found that there was no film in it. I had used up the last few photographs on the spool because I had wanted to have my holiday photographs developed quickly. I will now have no record of that precious moment.

My experience with hedgehogs is limited. I am sad when I see them flattened on the roads of our island. They have a curious disregard for motor cars—I imagine that hedgehog parents have a hard time teaching their offspring about looking "right, left and right again" before venturing to cross the road.

On the other hand they may do the drill and yet not be able to cross the road in time for hedgehogs do not have a ready turn of speed.

As I said goodnight to the hedgehogs at the gate, I found myself hoping that *they* would survive the dangers of our roads. Even my valley which is narrow and steep has motorists who hurtle down it with little regard for these creatures who want their share of God's world too.

When the Signal is weak. . .

I have bought a new second-hand television set.

I have a reputation for always buying new second-hand goods! They are, I argue, new to me so the expression is quite correct!

The new set was a vast improvement on the old friend who had served me well for ten years. I bought that set in 1976 so that my mother could see Wimbledon in colour. I felt it might be Gran's last Wimbledon and I was glad that she saw it before she died six months later.

The new set behaved very well until last month when it developed a disease which I was unable to cure. The picture was blurred and unsatisfactory, clear symptoms of trouble within.

I am not the sort of person to admit that I knew nothing about the technology of television, so with the instruction booklet in my hand, I set about the job of acting as the TV doctor. This differs from the Radio doctor only in the type of patient under treatment.

The book itself provided a considerable challenge. The variety of languages which the manufacturers had decided to use meant that the English instructions were fairly terse. An hour later, as a result of my ministration, the picture was worse and I was wondering whether to kick the infernal machine (as my father would have done. He was an engineer who frequently kicked the car when it would not start).

Thinking of my father reminded me that I had a very good professional TV engineer so I telephoned for help. I was, fortunately, not in when he called for his diagnosis would have embarrassed me. He left a note stating that he had sent for the aerial erector.

I dashed out of the cottage and looked up at the roof. The aerial was lying flat on its back having surrendered to the high wind. I kicked myself mentally for not having realised why the signal was weak.

There is a modern Chinese proverb relevant to this sort of incident:-

When the signal is weak—check that you are in touch with the source of all power.

The Umbrella Man

Every time I see the road sign which shows a poor man who cannot get his umbrella up, I smile and think of Ruth. The signs are all over our island as there are presently so many roads under repair. If the Main Roads Department in the United Kingdom and Jersey are under the impression that the sign shows a man digging then I can assure the authorities concerned that Ruth and I and all the people we have told about it, think differently.

When Ruth drew my attention to this poor man with umbrella trouble, she must have been about seven years old. (She is now adult and therefore much wiser). However, coming home from school one day, she found that the "road men" had decided to dig up part of the road outside the gate in the outskirts of Bristol where Ruth lived with her family. The men had brought their tools and their little hut, but then decided to go off for a cup of tea or whatever road men do to pass the time. They erected their "road under repair" sign before they left and Ruth came home to see the sign outside her gate.

She rushed into the house, announced to the family, and to me as I happened to be there at the time, "There's a picture of a poor man who cannot get his umbrella up outside our gate." It took her a little time to convince us that we must go and see the sign for ourselves but as soon as we saw it we agreed with Ruth. Up to that moment I had thought it depicted a man digging, but how wrong I was! Every time I see the road sign now, I wish the man would get his umbrella up and go away!

Two people can look at a picture and form quite a different impression of what the artist intended to convey.

Two people can face a situation and react to it in different ways.

Sometimes we can read a text or a motto and find it means differing things for different people.

This comes from an old calendar.

The difference between the lucky and the unlucky pedestrian is that the lucky ones get the brakes.

Too busy?

I was backing my car into a parking space when I saw him in my mirror. He was reading something intently and he was so engrossed in it that he barely looked up as I guided my car into the kerb.

The postman emerged from the house and I realised that the man was reading a newly-delivered letter. After I had adjusted my parking disc to the correct time and locked my car, I set off for my appointment. The man continued to read and I could see as I passed him, that it was a closely written letter of several pages that he had in his hand.

At a guess I would say that the letter which this elderly man was reading came from some member of his family and probably contained news of the family. Perhaps a grandchild had done well at school or maybe another baby was on the way. It could even have contained news of someone who was in hospital. The man was reading his letter with the concentration of someone for whom the written word was an unfamiliar means of communication, but the news was obviously important. As I walked past him, I brushed his arm.

"I'm sorry," I said apologetically. He never looked up. I do not think he was even aware of the brief encounter.

I will never know who wrote the letter or whether the news it contained was good or bad. The man was someone I had never seen before and I may never see again. Yet I have thought about him a great deal for he was so totally absorbed in his letter.

Letters are sometimes the only way of keeping in touch with old friends. Like praying, letter-writing is a discipline which, if neglected, can ultimately break a relationship. If you have lost touch with a friend, why not write today? If you have lost touch with God, why not re-establish the link?

If you are too busy to keep in touch with your friends or with God, you are too busy.

Rollers

The three small figures, duffle-coated and gum-booted, eyed the grass slope for a few moments. Then without exchanging a word they climbed to the top and one by one began to roll down, past the granite commemorative stone, down the steep slope until, breathless and pink-cheeked, they landed at the bottom.

I do not imagine that the architects and planners of the tall flats realised as they landscaped the gardens how successful they had been. The grass slope is perfect for rolling down and I can witness indeed to the enjoyment of three small rollers.

I could speak as an expert witness for I can vividly recall the pleasure that rolling down a slope can bring to the very young. I remember a very steep grass brae covered with primroses. To go from the top to the bottom, gathering momentum, was an exciting experience. I can recall too the reprimand I received on that bright Scottish day when the grass stains were found on our kilts.

Not many years ago I had myself to deal with a small boy who found the granite wall at the beach almost equally irresistible. The almost total destruction of a pair of trousers was only a mild deterrent compared with the pleasure of sliding down towards the damp sand.

I wonder if my three small friends were in trouble when they got home. I have a feeling that the wet grass would leave tell-tale marks on small trousers. If an exasperated mother anywhere is reading this, may I commend this little prayer to her?

Bless them God, now safe in bed,
the lights are out, the prayers are said.
A word in passing just to Thee —
Bless all tired mothers such as me.

The Glory of Life

"The wedding is off." I had been talking about the approaching wedding of the daughter of a mutual friend and the news took me aback.

Apparently two days before the wedding the arrangements were cancelled. We sat discussing, for a moment or two, the disruption which is caused when a wedding is cancelled at the last minute. Parents who have had to cope with such a situation will know only too well how much work is involved when this happens. There are presents to return, guests to alert, the church and reception arrangements to cancel, etc. It can be a highly charged emotional situation.

There are the customary words of comfort which one murmurs at the time. "Better to have discovered your mistake before than after the wedding," is the phrase which springs most readily to the lips as a tear-stained bride or a distraught groom pacing the floor. Some doubts are resolved after marriage but very often the doubts become certainties if a course is pursued which is wrong.

Just occasionally I have been asked by someone who thinks that he or she is "in love" how to assess the depth of feeling. Before indulging in any sort of final commitment, it is obviously better to know if the feeling one has for someone else is genuine and likely to last.

An old aunt used to tell me in the flighty days of my youth "Do not marry the one you love most but marry the one who loves you most." I remember pooh-poohing the advice at the time but I am not so sure now.

There is a poem called The Glory Of Life which expresses my aunt's point of view. I do not know the author.

The glory of life is to love, not to be loved
To serve, not to be served
To be a strong hand in the dark
To another in time of need
To be a cup of strength to any soul
In a crisis of weakness
This is to know the glory of life.

Qualifications

At this time of the year students who have finished their degree courses are filling up job applications and enclosing their CVs in the hope that their qualifications will impress future employers. Having listed the A-levels and the O-levels most applicants sit back hoping that they will at least get an interview.

Sometimes qualifications seem a little sparse, and school-leavers suck their pens as they try to see what a future employer really requires of them.

Those who are older and changing jobs find the problems just as hard. Giving an account of the jobs one has done can be daunting. Enclosing references occasionally helps but not all employers are generous in their praise, especially if an employee leaves an employer in the lurch.

What advice should be given to the job seeker?

I came across one man's description of his abilities when he was applying for the post of City Planner. He described himself as painter, architect, philosopher, poet, composer, sculptor, athlete, mathematician, inventor and anatomist. Not surprisingly he got the job of City Planner. Leonardo da Vinci, who lived from 1452-1519, had not exaggerated the situation when he gave his list of qualifications. It is a matter of interest however that da Vinci was not acknowledged in his lifetime as the genius recognised by subsequent generations.

I think most of us know our own limitations and are probably reluctant to try to impress others with abilities which we know we do not possess. School and university give us paper qualifications, but it is experience which makes us wiser.

For all who are going to new jobs, for those who are setting off into an unfamiliar world, I commend St Patrick's prayer.

May the strength of God pilot us
May the power of God preserve us.
May the wisdom of God instruct us.
May the hand of God protect us. . .
May Christ be with us, Christ before us,
Christ in us, Christ over us.

Things undone

When I was at the airport recently meeting some friends, I noticed with admiration the relaxed expressions on the faces of the visitors who were arriving on holiday. None of them seemed to have that anxious pre-occupied look which I always feel is *my* portion for the first twenty-four hours of my holiday. I believe many people suffer from a similar anxiety neurosis at the start of the annual break.

For me it all became more concrete when I saw a television programme which was a re-run of one of Tony Hancock's masterpieces. He had returned from his annual holiday to find he had forgotten to cancel the delivery of milk, bread and papers. The final scene was a great explosion which took place when he entered the kitchen. The gas tap had been left on during his absence.

Until that TV episode, I had never really allowed my imagination to dwell on the effect of a house flooded with milk, barricaded with loaves of bread and covered in a sea of unread newspapers. Now I find I spend anxious moments checking that everything is switched off and hoping desperately that I have remembered to cancel all the daily orders.

In the prayer of general confession which is part of our worship, we ask God's forgiveness for our forgetfulness and our failures. The words rightly remind us of our neglect of the things which should be important to us.

We have left undone things which we ought to have done and we have done those things which we ought not to have done.

Ladybird, Ladybird

"Shut your eyes and hold out your hand," said my young companion. He was stretched out beside me on the lawn enjoying the sunshine.

I eyed him suspiciously for a moment. The years have taught me to tread warily when this particular request is made.

I can still remember with a shiver the jellyfish which I once innocently grasped on a hot afternoon on the beach. There was too the unpleasant memory of the hairy caterpillar which I took from another small boy. It was only natural that I should hesitate this time.

As I closed my eyes and prayed that it would not be a rude awakening I thought what the worst experience could be. Slugs are my particular dread. The sight of a well-nourished slug falling out of lettuce leaves is something which I find hard to bear. I hoped that I was not going to be presented with one of these.

As I opened my eyes I had a pleasant surprise, there on my hand was a ladybird, my favourite insect. Perfectly shaped, artistically coloured and beautifully marked, the ladybird seems to me to have no vices. As I laid her gently on the grass, I felt the sense of pleasure which these tiny creatures always give me.

Albert Schweitzer's philosophy about the sanctity of life is something which I can understand when it comes to the ladybird. I suppose that if I were a very great philosopher like Schweitzer, I would be able to achieve a similar feeling about the importance of slugs.

The prayer that Schweitzer wrote as a boy sums up his feelings about the reverence of life:-

*O Heavenly Father protect and bless all things that have breath;
guard them from all evil and let them sleep in peace.*

Clear Vision

I made a very minor New Year Resolution this year. To my
surprise I have so far succeeded in keeping it. I decided and
resolved to clean my spectacles every morning before getting
up.

Now this may not seem to be an earth-shattering resolution
to all those who have greater battles to fight. However long
ago, I resolved that it was better to achieve a minor success
than to find myself beaten in a battle against superior forces.

I am therefore cleaning the spectacles every morning with the
little cloth so generously supplied by the optician.

For the whole of my spectacles-wearing life I have had friends
who have offered to clean my seeing aids because they felt that,
through a mist of dust and face powder, the world must have
seemed clouded. They were quite right but I was so used to
the view I had that I could only feel surprise and gratitude
when the spectacles were handed back bright and shining. The
view had changed remarkably.

One always receives surprises when we look through a pane
of glass if it is clean. Windows can get very dirty when the
weather is bad or when there is a lot of dust about. I became
used to my cottage windows being totally obscured by road
dust when the main drains were being laid down the valley
where I live. When the work was completed and I could clean
the windows, I was staggered by the uninterrupted view. My
spectacle resolution has given me a similar enjoyment.

Is there a moral to this spectacles-cleaning resolution? Yes, it has made me realise that to see through a glass darkly is a frustrating experience though it is one which we all experience on our spiritual journey. It is good to know that one day we will see clearly.

In *Good News for Modern Man*, there is a slightly different translation of the well-loved passage in First Corinthians, chapter 13, verse 12:

What we see now is like the dim image in a mirror; then we shall see face to face. What I know now is only partial; then it will be complete, as complete as God's knowledge of me.

Postcards

The shops which sell postcards find their business booms in the summer. In the winter such shops hide the cards which portray beaches bathed in sunshine with bronzed figures disporting themselves on the sands.

Some shops cater for tourists with more artistic tastes and they sell cards with spectacular views of the sun setting over Gorey Castle or a "still-life" of a cluster of lobster pots which might attract the more discerning.

There are, of course, the vulgar cards which, from time to time, have been the choice of those immature tastes. I can remember one 13-year old boy who I had staying with me, who purchased a selection of these cards which I felt would make the postmen blush. He assured me that his sister would find the card he had chosen extremely amusing but he did take my advice about the one he had chosen for his grandmother. It was vulgar beyond belief and I felt it would not gladden the heart of an elderly relative.

I confiscated that one and paid for a view postcard which I felt would be more suitable Granny material. I tore up the offending postcard with some relief.

While on the subject of postcards, I can recall some years ago, when I was holidaying in the Outer Hebrides, finding myself at a loss in a tiny shop in North Uist. I had gone into the shop to buy a postcard and was handed a box of somewhat early examples of postcard art.

Not only were they of an early vintage but they all portrayed places unconnected with North Uist. There was, for example, a fine picture of the Coolins of Skye and a view of Inverness, the gateway to the Highlands. There was even a photograph of the ferry at Kyle of Lochalsh.

I asked the girl behind the counter if she had any postcards of North Uist. "We only have postcards of other places" she said with that air of finality which precluded any further conversation. I left the shop puzzled by her remark and postcardless.

I have since that time bought hundreds of postcards from all sorts of exotic places. Yet best of all I remember the little shop in North Uist where all the postcards were of "other places." The little shop was in an idyllic setting in a beautiful wild island which would have given photographers great scope for their cameras. Yet, the postcards were all of "other places."

Perhaps we sometimes look wistfully at "other places" and do not always see the beauty under our very noses.

The world is charged with the grandeur of God.
Gerard Manley Hopkins

Welcome!

I almost lost my heart one summer to Monsieur Pussey. It was touch and go really. If there are those who sniff contemptuously at the mere mention of holiday romances, then let them sniff!

The *entente cordiale* was very *cordiale* indeed as far as I was concerned. It happened up there in the mountain auberge just below a ski resort and just above the little hamlet where I spent fourteen halcyon Pyrennean days.

The object of my affections was the patron of the little inn where we had a delicious Sunday lunch which lasted for the requisite number of hours that French people sensibly allocate to the sacred art of eating.

M. Pussey sat throughout the meal at an open charcoal grill fire amongst his customers. It was a very hot August Sunday and the little auberge was very hot.

M. Pussey was cooking lamb cutlets and a rather large type of sausage. The latter I did not venture to taste. He laughed and joked with all of us diners and, as the sweat poured off his brow, there were little sizzling noises as it hit the hot charcoal.

He had, sadly for me, a wife and two handsome daughters who brought him the raw ingredients and returned when he had cooked them appetisingly on his grill.

Throughout the hours of the meal, he kept up a cheerful badinage with us all and at the same time rescued charred cutlets and sizzling sausages from the flame.

We did not exchange many words, M. Pussey and I, but I admired him enormously for he had showed the sort of warmth of greeting to all who came under his roof which I found quite endearing.

I imagine most innkeepers, restaurateurs and hoteliers are, at times, not overjoyed to see their customers. Recently in Jersey I had a similar welcome from a restaurant owner not a million miles from my cottage but I am afraid that I have been in other Jersey establishments where I have not felt the warmth of welcome which M. Pussey afforded me.

It is not just the owner of a hotel or restaurant who should make guests feel welcome. It should be our privilege at all times to make those who step into our homes feel their coming has made us glad.

Did not the writer of the letter to the Hebrews give one good reason for writing "Welcome" on the mat? He wrote:-

"Do not forget to entertain strangers, for by doing so people have entertained angels without knowing it."

Hebrews 13, verse 2 (NIV)

Plain Words

I have a great affection for the American people, largely, I suppose, because I have a Californian family through my marriage. My visit last time to the Garden State was all delight and my encounters with some of the members of my family whom I had not met, were certainly stimulating occasions.

One of my young relatives had a very colourful way of expressing himself while using the minimum number of words. I can recall on one occasion I was showing him a pair of jeans which I had bought for 50 cents at a Thrift Shop.

For those unfamiliar with the pleasures of Saturday thrift shop forays, there is a whole new sphere of experience still to be enjoyed. But to revert to Adam (for that is his name), and my fifty cent jeans, I asked him if he approved of my new purchase. He looked me up and down and said softly, "You going to a flood?"

I looked down at my legs and saw that the jeans were perhaps slightly shorter than the ones which he was wearing. I got the point and spent the afternoon letting the hem down.

In the American Oxford Dictionary there are many examples of words which our cousins use but which are unfamiliar to us. There is, for example, a vast range of culinary expressions. Asking for eggs "sunny-side up" means you do not want them fried on both sides as opposed to "easy over" which means having the egg fried on both sides. Incidentally, if offered a "bagel" it is all right to take one if you happen to like hard ring-shaped bread rolls!

It is sometimes said by those outside the church that the language which churchgoers use is totally unfamiliar and incomprehensible. This accusation may be true but some statements from the Scriptures are very plain indeed. Who, for example, could improve upon the old Psalmist's description of God in the 23rd Psalm?

The Lord is my Shepherd.

Bath-time for the Birds

I have recently added another facility to my garden. It is for my feathered friends and I think they are appreciating the gesture.

The second-hand bird-bath and the cement kerbs which form a circle make a pleasant feature and it should be a delight to the birds.

Until I had provided a bird-bath, I did not realise how popular bathing is with birds. I have to refill the little bath very frequently for the birds seem to be like schoolboys after a game of rugby— determined to splash the bathwater all over the bathroom.

Selfishly I placed the bird-bath in a secret corner of the garden which can be viewed by me when sitting in the Granary. The Granary, which is named after my beloved mother who is always known as Gran, is the room in which I write. The bird-bath is only visible to me; passers-by do not have the private view of bathtime that I have.

The swallows skim past the bath with difficulty for the secret garden is tree-lined and they have not got much of a runway for their flights. In May the bluebells flank the new area and the lilac tree provides a pretty foreground for the bird-bathing section.

The lilac tree distinguished itself this year for I cut off some low branches to make a wigwam for the sweet peas which I planted in April. The lilac branches were obviously surprised by their new role in life but they decided that they would show the sweet peas not only how to climb but how to blossom.

I had therefore a lilac-flowering wigwam and regretted that the sweet peas were too tardy to see what the lilac tree had provided for their delight.

There is an inscription on a sun-dial in Wakehurst Place in Sussex which Francis Gay quotes in one of his friendship books:-

Give fools their gold and knaves their power. Let fortunes' bubbles rise and fall. Who sows a field or trains a flower or plants a tree is more than all.

Nudge-bars

I saw an advertisement for a "nudge-bar" the other day. This is not a chocolate-covered confection but a motoring accessory. Presumably, in a motoring context, a nudge-bar would have many uses.

One could nudge another car while parking in a limited space. One might nudge the odd pedestrian who crossed one's path regardless of life or limb. The garage door which invariably blows shut on a rainy night could be nudged open with one of these handy devices.

I do hope that my ideas for the use of the nudge-bar will not cause motoring experts to shatter my dream about the use of the nudge-bar by telling me what their real purpose is.

Apart from my imaginative uses for motor car nudge-bars, I can think of nudge-bars which might be fitted to one's person.

For example the Christmas cake is not yet made and not likely to be unless someone nudges me in the direction of the shop-up-the-road where I am provided with the ingredients each year without my having to be specific about the amount of fruit, flour and so on.

Our shop caters for the simple-minded like me. The super-market is no substitute for shoppers without a clue about what they require.

I need a nudge-bar to remind me to write long overdue letters.

I need a nudge-bar to remind me to visit shut-in friends and from time to time to stir me into activity.

I need a nudge-bar to remind me, that, when my temper

rises and my patience becomes exhausted, the Christian virtues of patience, gentleness and compassion ought to be uppermost at such times.

Remind me O God of my need of Thee. Stir me into activity for Thee. Help me to reflect Thy Love in this Thy world.

Hodja's Jokes

I received a book for Christmas entitled *"202 Jokes of Nasreddin Hodja."* As I had never heard of the gentleman in question, and thought at first that his name must be an anagram of some more likely name, I dipped into the book with interest.

I learned that Nasreddin Hodja is one of the most loved and celebrated personalities, not only of Turkey, but of the entire Middle East. He was born in Horto, a village in the province of Sivrihisar, Turkey, in 1208. His father was a Moslem priest of the village and Hodja lived during the reign of the powerful and terrible Sultan Timur Leng.

As well as possessing a keen sense of humour, he lived the life of a good man and a scholar. The name Nasreddin means "Helper of the Faith" and Hodja was an honorary title given to him because of his scholarship. Hodjas were allowed to wear special white turbans to show their status in society.

I gleaned all this from the introduction to the book and then turned to the contents. The jokes are all listed alphabetically and have much of the wisdom of folk lore in them.

I liked the joke entitled "Cheap Donkeys". Apparently every

market day Hodja would take a donkey to market and sell it for a price well below that of his competitors. One day a rich merchant asked him how he could undercut everyone.

The merchant said "I have my servants steal hay from the farmer and I force my servants to keep the donkeys without paying them, yet your prices are lower than mine!"

"Well that's understandable," replied Hodja. "You steal food and labour. I steal donkeys."

It is difficult to assess whether the donkey merchant or Hodja was the bigger thief. We are not called upon to judge the actions of other people as a rule.

I read recently of a sentence which has some bearing on the judging of others and I have no doubt Hodja will have some pithy story about that. The aphorism is attributed to Arnold Bennett.

It is well when one is judging a friend to remember that he is judging you with the same god-like and superior impartiality.

Strained Relationships

It is an extraordinary fact that couples who have lived together for years and then get married suddenly find the relationship is strained. I have been told this by sociologists, psychiatrists, psychologists and counsellors.

The breakdown in marriage of those who have lived happily

together "in sin" (as it used to be called) is apparently very alarming. Marriage guidance counsellors find frequent examples of this new problem.

What is it which makes the binding contract of marriage so different from the looser contract between couples who have not been legally bound together?

I do not believe that relationships which are formed outside marriage stand the best chance of survival. I believe that making a commitment in the eyes of God is assuming a responsibility for each other which every couple should recognise.

It is strange, therefore, to learn that those who have lived happily outside marriage find that, when the commitment is made, the cracks appear in the relationship. Perhaps they were never mature enough to look at what is meant by a Christian attitude to marriage.

Marriages which fail end in the Divorce Courts. Relationships which end leave a sad feeling of failure in the hearts of those who feel bereft. This prayer sums up what many people feel as they survey the wreck of their lives:-

Lord — why did you allow this to happen to me? I had such high hopes and now I only have bitter memories of a marriage which no longer is — help me to pick myself up and look forwards. Not backwards over my shoulder. Let me not be bitter, God, for bitterness is self-destroying.

Signs of Intolerance?

I would like to think that as I grow older, I grow more tolerant.

When I was young I was totally convinced that I was right on most occasions. If this gives the impression that I was a pig-headed, self-opinionated person, I think that would be, roughly, my own assessment of my younger self.

There are those who may think that I have changed little. However, I am aware that I no longer hold all the views that I once held. Furthermore I now realise that other people are not only entitled to their opinions but are quite frequently correct in the points of view which they hold.

This week I am a year older and that is why I have come to this watershed in my development. I am beginning to see the writing on the wall and, if I cannot read it too clearly, it is the fault of the oculist and not a lack of understanding on my part.

The man whom I dearly loved told me once that hardening of the arteries is sometimes accompanied by hardening of one's opinions as one grows older. There is little that we can do to prevent our arteries hardening but there is a good deal that we can do to prevent our minds hardening. The generation gap is widened when we, who are older, judge those who are younger, by our standards.

I met a young man recently who from his earring to his tight jeans, looked like any other youngster. When I talked to him, however, I discovered that, under the veneer of rather exotic gear and the language of his peers he had a deep sense of vocation about helping others less privileged than himself.

I could so easily have written him off as a potential thug or hooligan by his outward appearance but instead he was intent upon following a career with little monetary reward but devoted to helping the unfortunate in society.

This week, when I am a year older, I would pray that my mind will not harden with my arteries and that my friends will point out to me when I begin to show the signs of intolerance which sometimes indicate the ageing process.

I found a wonderful quotation the other day. It happens to apply to religious differences but it can equally apply to all disagreements.

The broad-minded see the truth in different religions; the narrow-minded see only the differences.

Lao-tze

Fork-lifts

I have only recently begun to appreciate fork-lifts, I have, of course, been familiar with ordinary forks for most of my life. The table variety and the pitch fork are, in their spheres, essential pieces of equipment.

But fork-lifts are less known to me. The idea of a lift or a hoist is not a novel one for man, in his very early days, devised primitive ways of lifting heavy objects.

Incidentally the introduction of lifts into certain shops, libraries and blocks of flats makes life so much easier for shoppers, book-borrowers, flat-dwellers and deliverers. Before our own library had a lift I was wont to pant like a goldfish when going to change my books. I am happy to say that the only exercise needed now is mental stimulation! I can never remember the name of one author whose book I would enjoy borrowing.

But to revert to the subject of the fork-lift.

I must admit that this piece of machinery appeals to me. I first appreciated its tremendous value when I saw a number of these machines in use in the store-rooms of one of our largest supermarkets. From floor to ceiling the heavy cartons had been hoisted and stacked by these mechanical wonders and the men who operated them told me they could not imagine what life would be like without them. The fork-lift must have proved itself in many industries, both in time and labour-saving.

At the airport fork-lifts play an important part in getting cargo and luggage into the aircraft. They are also used sometimes to lift disabled wheelchair passengers into the planes and that is an important role.

As I stood at the airport watching one of man's modern toys in action, I found myself coveting a machine which would lift things for *me*.

I remember once admitting an urge to own a steam roller. Fortunately these machines went off our roads in time to save me from certain imprisonment. Stealing a road roller must be a heinous crime and I have no doubt pinching a fork-lift would be viewed equally gravely by the powers that be. I hope no one is foolish enough to leave a fork-lift outside my gate! When a steam roller was left there some years ago, it took all my will-power to resist starting it up and driving it away.

Most people have too much will power. It's won't power they lack.

Dents and Lumps

There are two very small dimples on the bonnet of my comparatively new car. I do not think that they are worth a visit to the panel beater, for you can only see them in a certain light.

I have tried to remove them with a rubber plunger which I use for unstopping my kitchen sink but the size of the suction cap is larger than the little dimples. So far I have had no success at all with the dents.

Worse than that, at one stage the rubber plunger took such a hold on the bonnet that if I had not been determined to hold my ground and get it off, I might be motoring everywhere with the kitchen sink-plunger on my car for the rest of its life.

I have not gone to the panel-beater as the two dimples scarcely merit such a visit. I would also be somewhat reluctant to have to explain how they came to be there in the first place.

Would a panel beater believe that they were actually caused by a television trolley?

I can imagine the look of disbelief on his face when such an explanation was offered! It would be difficult to explain that the TV trolley, which up to then had displayed no murderous intent, had decided to plunge from the rafters of my garage down on to my hapless head. Yes, it did hit *me* before landing on the car bonnet.

I had never done that trolley any harm and there was simply no excuse for its behaviour. Strangely my head reacted to the trolley in a quite different way from the car bonnet. I developed two small pigeon's egg type lumps, whereas the bonnet had the dimples. I suppose flesh and metal do react differently to similar circumstances.

It is not only flesh and metal which react differently to misfortune. People react differently too. Some laugh at minor misfortunes; others rage or weep.

We are, the dietician says, what we eat. We are, the Christian says, what we believe. So we react differently according to our differing viewpoints.

As Frederick Longbridge wrote:-

Two men look through the same bars —
One sees the mud, and one sees stars.
From A Cluster of Quiet Thoughts
Published by The Religious Tract Society

In the Valley of Sadness

Several of my friends have been walking through the dark valley of sadness recently.

In our journey through life we are walking along quite happily when, suddenly, we turn a corner and there is a dark valley that we had not expected to find on our route.

There was sunlight behind us and darkness in front of us. We had not been prepared for the valley which was not marked on our map.

There is no alternative but to go on. There is no turning back, so with leaden footsteps and heavy hearts, we plunge into the valley of sadness.

As we grope our way along the path we know that, although there will be light again at the other end as we climb out of the valley, the sunlight will never be quite as bright as it was before.

We each have different methods of dealing with our own dark valley routes. Some of us prefer to walk alone and rely on our own strength. Others hold on to those who have walked the way before and who know the agony of heart which such a journey entails.

There is no blueprint for such a journey. We have to struggle to find our own way through the valley of sadness and when we emerge we have an experience to share with others whose darkness is ahead of them.

There is an allegorical story of a man who dreamed he was

walking along the beach with his Lord. As he turned he noted that there were two sets of footprints in the sand. However, as the scenes of his life unfolded he noticed that when some portions of his life had been particularly agonising there was only one set of prints.

Realising that in his worst moments he had apparently been alone, he asked his Lord why He had abandoned him in his valleys of sadness.

Our Lord said:

My precious, precious child — I love you and would never leave you. During your times of trial and suffering when you see only one set of footprints, it was then that I carried you.

Cold Comfort

"I think I've got a cold coming." a friend of mine told me, with a sniff.

"There are a lot of colds about," I said in what I thought was a sympathetic response.

"It's not much comfort to know other people have got colds when you are feeling rotten yourself," was the unexpected reply.

The reply was unexpected because, in my experience, the knowledge that other people are suffering from similar ills and diseases has always been a comfort to me.

In Jersey, viruses have circular tendencies. You hear constantly that some particular virus, whether it affects stomach, liver, throat or wherever it chooses to situate itself, is "going round."

I like to think that I have a common complaint. If I am the only one with an illness or disease, there is a loneliness about the whole business.

Some time ago a friend of mine sent me a poem entitled "I'm fine." Here are the first and last lines of Mai Sherman's verse.

There's nothing whatever the matter with me
I'm just as healthy as I can be
I have arthritis in both my knees.
And when I walk I talk with a wheeze.
But I'm awfully well for the shape I'm in.
Now the moral is, as the tale we unfold—
That for you and me who are growing old,
It's better to say—I'm fine with a grin
than to tell everyone the shape we are in!

Alice

Alice's bed was sold for £1,600.

"Who is Alice?" you may well ask and I would have to reply that there is really only one Alice whose bed would fetch so much money.

The Alice in *Alice in Wonderland* was, of course, the girl in question and her adventures, *Through the Looking-glass* and Alice in Wonderland, have delighted generations of children. It was in Wonderland that she went to a mad tea-party and danced a lobster quadrille with a mock turtle and a gryphon. (I mention these facts lest memories need prompting).

Alice was the daughter of the Dean of Christchurch and the Liddell family were close friends of the Rev Charles Lutwidge Dodgson, a young Oxford don who was then a Lecturer in Mathematics.

Dodgson took as his *nom de plume* "Lewis Carroll" when he wrote down and published the stories he used to tell the little Liddell girls when they were together. Alice was his favourite listener for she was a rather solemn, attentive child. She always prompted him when he faltered in his story-telling role.

Carroll wrote for older readers as well as for his young friends. One poem written three days after seeing Holman Hunt's picture "The Finding of Christ in the Temple," has revealing insights of a man in search for God. I particularly like his description of looking into the eyes of Christ in the painting.

Look into those deep eyes,
Deep as the grave, and strong with love divine.
Those tender pure and fathomless mysteries,
That seem to pierce through mine.

Retirement

One of the awful side-effects of unemployment is boredom. If you have been programmed, for the best part of your life, to a work pattern, the loss of a job through redundancy or retirement can be a very difficult experience.

"The trouble is the week-ends," a friend of mine said to me recently. He had just retired from a very busy life. "I mean I used to look forward to the week-ends, but now frankly the week-ends are the worst of all because they are no different from the rest of the week."

I could see instantly what he meant for he had, of course, spent a life which was geared to having time off only when he was on holiday, or on Saturdays and Sundays. Then out of the blue every day was Saturday and he was finding it difficult to come to terms with a life of retirement.

His experience is not nearly as hard, however, as the man who finds he has been prematurely retired through no fault of his own. This happened to another friend of mine who found himself made redundant in his early forties when the house mortgage and the children's needs were very demanding. A year out of work with the agony of trying for a job which hundreds of other applicants were fighting to get, was a year he will never forget.

Is there advice for those who are newly retired or compulsorily retired? There are magazines and journals which do make helpful suggestions. In them well-known writers give their own experience of planning leisure time. I am not one of these writers for I cannot write from first-hand experience, but only from my observations of the experiences of others.

One piece of advice was given to me and I pass it on. It was to make the week-ends different from the rest of the week.

One way would of course be to go to church on Sundays. You have never been since you went to Sunday School? Well, why not "give it a whirl" this week-end?

CH . . . CH means nothing unless UR in it.

Slogans

There is a very special art in writing slogans and captions.

Many years ago I remember hearing that Selfridges, that great London store, had filled every one of their Oxford Street windows with refrigerators.

There were fridges of every size and description, and on each window there was a very small notice. Each had the simple message "We Selfridges"—We sell-fridges.

I have remembered that advertisement for many years because the neatness of the slogan appealed to me.

When I was in Berkeley, California some years ago, I noticed a small bus which was named "The Humphrey Go-Bart." The bus plied between Berkeley and the Bay area and the letters BART stood for the transport system which linked Berkeley with San Francisco. The play on the name of the well-known actor appealed to my sense of fun.

A friend who was holidaying in Yorkshire, had seen a notice in an inn with low beams which made her chuckle. Affixed to the beams was the simple statement—"Duck or Grouse."

When I heard of that simple piece of advice, I thought that it could be applied to other situations in life. You can avoid hitting your head by ducking or you can refuse to take advice and grumble when you get a headache.

It is easier to give advice than to take it. I usually regret giving advice when I have not been asked to do so. I fear that the temptation to tell other people what to do frequently assails me.

I have a little motto hanging in the Granary and I often glance at this good piece of advice. I offer it as a statement of my experience in life.

In order to get from what was to what will be you have to go through what is.

We need Support

The Montana Clematis was better than ever this year. I cut it back but not too severely at the appropriate time last year—after it had flowered—and it rewarded me for my pains.

It covered the front of the cottage almost completely. A new tendril struggling to catch on to the sitting-room window proved to me that a clematis, given the right support, will do its level best to hold on.

There are times in our lives when we need support. Naturally when we are small and learning to walk, we have to have a helping-hand with our first hesitant steps.

It is an incredible step of faith for a child to walk unaided for the first time. It is only when confidence is total that the first unsupported steps are taken.

As we grow up there are other times in our lives when we need support. The uncertain years of adolescence can throw up enormous problems of insecurity. So many teenage problems are due to lack of support. Parental support is particularly needed.

During the early and middle years we achieve some measure of independence and attempt to paddle our own canoes, rejecting offers of help. As old age approaches, we become less independent and have to rely on the support of those who are younger and stronger.

Throughout our lives, we have God's help in every difficulty. His support never fails. In the Church of Scotland in which I grew up this prayer nearly always formed part of the evening service. It always comforted me:-

O Lord support us all the day long of this troublous life, until the shadows lengthen and the evening comes, and the busy life is hushed and the fever of life is over and our work done. Then Lord in thy mercy grant us safe lodging, a holy rest and peace at the last.

Attributed to J.H. Newman, possibly based on an earlier traditional prayer.

Bonfires

I love making bonfires. I have always enjoyed the smell of wood smoke and the cheerful crackling of a fire burning out of doors.

At one period of my life, I was actually paid to light bonfires.

For two months I was employed by a timber firm to clear the remains of a forest that had been cut down during the war and it was a time of rare delight. It was hard work certainly but it was a lovely hot summer. Though it meant toiling up the hillside in Aberdeenshire, it seemed an easy way to earn a living.

There were four of us employed by the timber firm and we camped in a lovely spot near our field of operation. As we were paid by the acreage we cleared, there was no pressure upon us to work regular hours.

We rarely started before midday. Towards evening the problem of getting the massive fires out before blackout was considerable. I still waken up with the cry of the village policeman ringing in my ears I heard so often in those far off days.

"The hill's on fire — get up!"

We used to tumble out of our sleeping bags, harness ourselves to the water carts and run, like Chinese coolies of the olden days, up the hillside. Once on the hill we would use the stirrup pump to try to control the fire beating out the persistent flames with spades. Fire spreads very quickly under heather.

Our feelings were always a little mixed when we fought the hill fire. Obviously the policeman, representing law and order and also very conscious of the desirability of not guiding enemy bombers to the village, was anxious that we got the fire under control quickly. We, on the other hand, knew that no enemy bomber had ever been in the vicinity.

The unexpected fire was also a bonus for us. A good fire could clear more ground in a night than we could achieve in two days. We were paid (as I recall) £2 an acre and, in a good week, we could make £4. That on our reckoning at that time was riches indeed.

Last week I lit a bonfire in the garden. As the smoke curled upwards, I was transported in imagination back to that Scottish hillside and I found myself being thankful for so many happy memories.

Thank you God for so many happy memories. May I remember the happy times when I am walking through the valley of despair.

Plumbago

"My plumbago has been wonderful this year" I said to a friend.

"I'm glad to hear it," she said brightly. "I didn't know you had it."

"I've had it for some years now," I said happily, "and it is an absolute joy."

My friend looked at me in astonishment. "Most people would not describe it as a joy."

"It's all over the front of the cottage and I suppose the bush is about twelve feet high and covered with those lovely pale blue clusters." I continued.

She stopped in her tracks and turned to look at me.

"What on earth *are* you talking about?" she asked in bewilderment.

"My plumbago," I said "what are *you* talking about?"

"Great heavens" she said "I thought you were on about your *lumbago!*"

I burst out laughing and admitted that, although the *plumbago* was rampant, *lumbago* had not so far attacked me in the lumbar region.

All this led to my friend telling me that she was a little hard of hearing and found that she did occasionally get hold of the wrong end of the stick. It meant that she had to concentrate rather hard to hear properly. Facing the speaker was a distinct help. As we had been walking along side by side, the 'p' of plumbago had been lost in the air.

I am told by those who work among the deaf that one of the hardest things which they have to bear is the lack of sympathy which they get over their affliction. Blind people attract friends but deaf people often seem to repel the unthinking and the unfeeling.

Those of us who can hear should listen carefully to what is being said. We all switch off at times because the conversation bores us. We learn this art at an early age for children soon learn the knack of ignoring adult conversation which they find boring. As we grow older, we have to remind ourselves that we can hurt someone very deeply by only listening with half an ear to what is being said.

Christ told his followers that they were blessed because they could see and hear the truth of the Gospel. It is still true for us today so we do well to heed his words:-

But blessed are your eyes because they see and your ears because they hear.

Matthew 13, verse 16 (NIV)

From little to large

The hydrangeas have borne the brunt of my annual foray with the pruning shears. I look forward to the day when I can get my own back on the hydrangeas for I cast baleful glances at them for most of the summer months.

Other people's hydrangeas may be small bushes with blooms of various colours ranging from deep red to glorious purple. Our hydrangeas are enormous, wild-looking plants which tower above us. The blooms, despite treatment from various chemicals, are a persistent off-white with a sickly green hue as if the treatment had induced a bilious attack.

I wait eagerly for the day when I can annually get my own back and cut them down to bare wooden stumps. I do this when the first buds form on the lower branches. I am therefore standing surrounded by foliage and blossoms which resemble the heads of decapitated enemies, lying at my feet.

I suppose the real answer would be to uproot these plants and start anew with a fresh species but I cannot bring myself to do this. I feel a reluctant admiration for them in their persistence and in their defiance of my colouring methods.

I remember a similar rhubarb forest in my childhood when the stalks were the width of small saplings and the leaves afforded shade to small children.

My husband, with whom I shared my life for too short a time, had a similar rhubarb forest in his garden so we used to compare notes about the way we had eaten our way through the forests of our childhood.

My hydrangeas and the rhubarb forests remind me of Christ's illustration of the Kingdom of God which he likened to a mustard seed which grows from a tiny seed to a plant on which birds may rest.

However small your faith, with His help it is sufficient.

Industrial Relations

A friend who receives the Scottish newspaper, the *Sunday Post*, (a paper much loved by exiled Scots as well as by those who live in the country of my birth), sent me a cutting from it recently.

It was printed by the newspaper at the time when the teachers' dispute was at its height.

It confirmed what I had always feared about the American attitude to the teaching profession of many years ago. I hope that, by now, the type of contract which a Wisconsin teacher had to sign in 1922 is a museum item only.

This is how it reads:

Miss . . . . agrees

* *Not to get married, otherwise this contract becomes null and void.*

* *Not to have company with men.*

* *To be home between the hours of 8 p.m. and 6 a.m. unless in attendance at school.*

* *Not to loiter in ice-cream stores.*

* *Not to leave town without the permission of the chairman of the trustees.*

* *Not to smoke cigarettes on pain of dismissal.*

* *Not to drink beer, wine or whisky.*

★ Not to ride in a carriage or automobile with any man except her brother or father.

★ Not to dye her hair.

★ Not to wear dresses more than two inches above the ankle.

★ To keep the school clean, to scrub the classroom floor at least weekly with soap and hot water.

★ To start the fire at 7 a.m. so the room will be warm at 8 a.m. when the children arrive.

★ Not to wear face powder, or mascara or paint the lips.

The salary for that Wisconsin teacher was $75 per month.

Happily industrial relations have improved greatly in the last 60 years, but there are certain fundamental things to be observed in every relationship, whether it be industrial, friendly or domestic agreement.

One of them, and one which we should remember, is this:-

God made man in His image so that we should be like Him. If we remember this we will not exploit or use other people for our own gratification.

An electrical Upset

It takes me longer to change a plug than it does to write my *Weekly Special* for the *Jersey Evening Post*.

I discovered this a few moments ago when I stopped typing

next week's contribution in order to mend the vacuum cleaner plug. The problem was simple. One of the leads had come adrift.

It took me only a matter of minutes to assemble my tools — two screwdrivers — for the rest it was just a matter of concentration.

The plug was a simple device, it had a fuse that lay across a little clamp. One leg of the clamp made up the part of the plug which fitted into the socket. I noted that the blue lead was adrift and started work. I found that more of the wire had to be exposed to get it into the little hole.

I then discovered that my tools were inadequate. Sadly, I cut too far into the covering and severed the wire. I then had to cut the brown covering so that the pieces were of equal length.

I will not go into what happened next. It must be obvious even to the inexpert electrician like me.

Eventually I got the two wires into their appropriate holes and tightened the screws. From then on it should have been child's play, but in the excitement of involuntarily shortening the wires, I had dropped the central screw which holds the plug together.

I spent some time crawling about on the carpet looking for the screw. The carpet in my sitting room is a highly patterned one. If the screw had been searching for an ideal hiding place, it would have chosen this floor covering in preference to any other carpet in the island.

Eventually I found it the hard way. I knelt on it! Biting back the tears which sprang to my eyes, I tightened up the screw.

It was then that I discovered however that I had reduced the number of legs on the plug from three to two. I undid the plug and restored it to its three-legged state.

Was it not an old Chinese philosopher who wrote

Although it may take a long time to achieve little, it is better to achieve little than to attempt nothing.

A Hedgehog in Transit

"You are without doubt, the only dog who can pick up a hedgehog," I said to Tovey.

This week Horace (or could it have been Henrietta?) Hedgehog — one of the two I had seen in an amorous encounter — returned. Tovey found the caller in the drive and gave it an involuntary walk round the policies.

Those born south of the Border may not realise that "policies", according to the dictionary, are the pleasure grounds of a Scottish mansion. In the case of my cottage and its grounds the word "policies" is somewhat pretentious, but I make no apology for its use for I like the word.

To revert to Horace/Henrietta, I rescued him/her from Tovey and put him/her in the Sanctuary Garden. That also sounds a little pretentious, but the Sanctuary Garden is the part of the policies into which no black dog may stray and where hedgehogs may drink a saucer of milk of an evening undisturbed.

I have to admit that I had my doubts as to whether

Horace/Henrietta would survive the involuntary ride in Tovey's mouth. It could not have been an enjoyable experience and certainly was an unplanned part of the hedgehog itinerary.

I suppose the situation was made just bearable by the fact that Tovey lost his top front teeth in another "Brief Encounter" with a tractor or horse.

Tovey was not able to describe that drama to me. The vet removed the broken teeth and, since that episode, Tovey has resembled an elderly gentleman who has forgotten to put in his dentures.

Horace/Henrietta is well and happy and drinks his/her milk nightly in the Sanctuary Garden.

Everyone ought to have a sanctuary or place of retreat where there is peace and an opportunity to be quiet.

And then the scholar said "speak of talking". And he answered, saying: "you talk when you cease to be at peace with yourself". Kahlil Gibran (The Prophet) published by Heinemann.

A Day at a Time

I have for a long time told people who come to me for advice to live a day at a time. They have a problem which seems insoluble. They look into the future which is totally dominated by the situation in which they find themselves and they are sorely burdened.

I nearly always advocate that they attempt to get through each day as it comes and try not to get weighed down by the problems of the uncertain nature of the future.

It is easy to give advice but hard to take it. I have lain awake at night worrying about things which have never happened. I have crossed bridges which no one has ever built, over rivers which have never existed. I have asked people for advice and ignored it. I am, I imagine, typical of most people.

I was interested to read a wonderful piece of advice from that marvellous organisation Alcoholics Anonymous. I found it in a magazine. And I have abstracted what seems to me to be the most helpful section of the advice given there:

Just for today I will try to live through this day only, and not tackle my whole life problem at once. I can do something for twelve hours that would appal me if I had to keep it up for a lifetime.

Just for today I will be happy. Most folks are as happy as they make up their minds to be.

Just for today I will adjust myself to what is, and not try to adjust everything to my own desires. I will take my luck as it comes and fit myself to it.

Just for today I will try to strengthen my mind. I will study. I will learn something useful. I will not be a mental loafer. I will read something that requires effort, thought and concentration.

Just for today I will exercise my soul in three ways. I will do somebody a good turn and not get found out — if anybody knows it will not count. I will do at least two things I don't want to do — just for exercise.

Just for today I will have a quiet hour all by myself and relax.

I will try to get a better perspective of my life. Just for today I will be unafraid.

Take no anxious thought for the morrow. In other words take life a day at a time.

THE WAY OF LOVE
by
Denis Duncan

Undated selections from January to June of
A Day at a Time

VICTORIOUS LIVING
by
Denis Duncan

Undated selections from July to December of
A Day at a Time

ARTHUR JAMES
One Cranbourne Road, London N10 2BT
4, Broadway Road, Evesham, Worcs. WR11 6BH

Phone and Fax 0386 6566   Fax 01 883 8307

Other devotional books in the Amulree Series
by
Denis Duncan

CREATIVE SILENCE
An exploration of silence
with twenty meditation outlines

LOVE, the Word that heals

Reflections on First Corinthians, Chapter 13

Available through all bookshops

ARTHUR JAMES
One Cranbourne Road, London N10 2BT
4, Broadway Road, Evesham, Worcs. WR11 6BH

Phone and Fax 0386 6566   Fax 01 883 8307

WILLIAM BARCLAY
books
from ARTHUR JAMES

THROUGH THE YEAR WITH WILLIAM BARCLAY
An inspirational thought for each day of the year
edited and introduced by Denis Duncan

EVERY DAY WITH WILLIAM BARCLAY
A further year's daily thoughts
edited and introduced by Denis Duncan

MARCHING ORDERS
Six months daily readings for younger people by William Barclay
edited and introduced by Denis Duncan

MARCHING ON
A further six months daily readings for younger people
by William Barclay
edited and introduced by Denis Duncan

SEVEN FRESH WINESKINS
William Barclay's exposition of Old Testament passages

ARTHUR JAMES' books by William Barclay, the most prolific
religious writer of modern times, are available from all
bookshops or, plus post and packing, from the publisher.

One Cranbourne Road, London N10 2BT
4, Broadway Road, Evesham, Worcs. WR11 6BH

ARTHUR JAMES'
Devotional Classics

GOD CALLING
over 2,000,000 copies sold, world-wide

GOD AT EVENTIDE
over 1,000,000 copies sold,world-wide

A TREASURY OF DEVOTION
GOD CALLING and GOD AT EVENTIDE in a presentation edition

GOD CALLING is also published in "de luxe"
and Large Print editions

ARTHUR JAMES
One Cranbourne Road, London N10 2BT
4, Broadway Road, Evesham, Worcs. WR11 6BH

A DAY AT A TIME
by
Denis Duncan

A thought and a prayer for
each day of a year

ARTHUR JAMES
One Cranbourne Road,
London N10 2BT

TELL THEM TO ME
by
Gwyn Filby

Stories of Jesus
in a contemporary setting

For school assemblies, women's meetings,
addresses, children's talks, youth clubs
etc.

ONLY £1.95

ARTHUR JAMES
One Cranbourne Road,
London N10 2BT